SUSTAINED TIMED WRITINGS

Fourth edition

Robert L. Grubbs, Ed.D.
Robert Morris College
Coraopolis, Pennsylvania

James L. White, Ed.D.
East Carolina University
Greenville, North Carolina

McGraw-Hill

New York, New York
Columbus, Ohio
Woodland Hills, California
Peoria, Illinois

Imprint 2002
Copyright © 1982 by Glencoe/McGraw-Hill. All rights reserved. Copyright © 1982, 1971, 1963, 1958 by McGraw-Hill, Inc. All rights reserved. Printed in the United States of America. Except as permitted under the United States Copyright Act, no part of this publication may be reproduced or distributed in any form or by any means, or stored in a database or retrieval system, without the prior written permission from the publisher. Send all inquiries to: Glencoe/McGraw-Hill, 21600 Oxnard Street, Suite 500, Woodland Hills, CA 91367-4906.

24 25 26   073/043   06 05 04 03

ISBN 0-07-025063-4

CONTENTS

Introduction IV

No.	Title of Selection	Page	Speed	Errors	Date	Speed	Errors	Date
1	September Delight	1						
2	The Night I Died	2						
3	Polly Pilsener	3						
4	Never Again	4						
5	The Singing Frogs	5						
6	Tomorrow	6						
7	My Forebear, the Teacher	7						
8	Godfather's Time	8						
9	The Legend of St. Nick	9						
10	Desire	10						
11	To Solve a Problem	11						
12	The Difference—About Twenty Years	12						
13	Rabbits and Coyotes	13						
14	A Potato Race	14						
15	The Lobster's New Suit	15						
16	Down the River of Time	16						
17	The Friendly Stream	17						
18	As It Was in the Beginning	18						
19	All Work and No Play . . .	19						
20	Pull	20						
21	Reading Is Fun	21						
22	The Fourth Dimension	22						
23	Research: Friction, Paints	23						
24	The "Craneberry"	24						
25	An Outdoor Hazard	25						
26	Bells	26						
27	Duffy's Spur	27						
28	Grabbing the Coattails	28						
29	The Poor Chameleon	29						
30	This Fable Teaches . . .	30						
The Sea								
31	Seasick and the Sea	31						
32	Sea Creatures	32						
Fishing								
33	Fishing on the Farm	33						
34	Fishing and Luck	34						
The Winner								
35	The Winner	35						
36	The Prize	36						
Success								
37	Goals and Performance	37						

Sponsoring Editor: Audrey Schmidt Rubin
Editing Supervisor: Fredric Dannen/Scott Kurtz
Design Supervisor: Sheila Granda
Production Supervisor: Avé Montero

No.	Title of Selection	Page	Speed	Errors	Date	Speed	Errors	Date
38	Success and the Technique of Living	38						
	Summer							
39	Carefree Days of Summer	39						
40	A Small Boy and Blueberries	40						
	Ice Cream							
41	First There Was Snow Ice	41						
42	Then There Was Ice Cream	42						
	Rules Of The Road							
43	Rules of the Road	43						
44	Do Unto Others	44						
	Bread							
45	Take Four Cups of Flour	45						
46	Then Add Some Yeast	46						
	The Management Game							
47	The Management Game	47						
48	More on the Management Game	48						
	The Supplies Department							
49	The Supplies Department	49						
50	More About the Supplies Department	50						
	Balsa							
51	Balsa, the Lightest Wood	51						
52	Balsa, the Insulator	52						
	Failure							
53	The Oversight	53						
54	Two Sure Things	54						
	The Owl							
55	A Need to Change	55						
56	Senior Owls	56						
	Lost							
57	Lost	57						
58	Lost and Found	58						
59	Lost or Mislaid	59						
	Cactus							
60	Cactus Country	60						
61	The Blooming Cactus	61						
62	Leave That Cactus Alone!	62						
	The Whale							
63	The Beginning of a Yarn	63						
64	A Boat and a Whale	64						
65	A Whale of a Yarn	65						
	Practice							
66	If at First . . .	66						
67	You Don't Succeed . . .	67						

CONTENTS

INTRODUCTION

The Purpose of This Book

If you are a typist, or are training to become one, this book has been published for you. You may use it with confidence for both profit and pleasure. It is intended to serve many purposes, some if not all of which may be precisely aligned with your own goals and needs.

The basic purpose of the book is implied in its name, Sustained Timed Writings. Within its covers are generous portions of typewriting matter that can be typed for sheer pleasure or to extend your ability to type rapidly and accurately for sustained intervals. It is straight-copy, timed-writing material — the kind of skill-building material that anyone can use to achieve fluency in typing, or to regain it if it has been lost.

Straight-copy timed writings are the most celebrated and frequently used teaching-testing device ever employed in the development of typewriting skill. With appropriate copy, the race against time provides the ingredients both for building and measuring the foundations of solid typing skill — speed, accuracy, endurance, and confidence in stroking the keyboard. In addition, the keyboard race provides an almost instantaneous assessment of personal accomplishment. Such instant feedback is a comfortable and effective spur to continued achievement. Moreover, the familiar words-a-minute score (WAM) is a standard appraisal gauge not only in the classroom but also in the office.

Preplanning Your Timed-Practice Sessions

Before you place the paper in your typewriter, establish a plan. Improvement in typing skill is achieved as much with

No.	Title of Selection	Page	Speed	Errors	Date	Speed	Errors	Date
68	Try, Try Again	68						
	English							
69	English? No Escape!	69						
70	English? Learn by Doing!	70						
71	English? The Easiest Way!	71						
	House Building							
72	Frame, Brick, or Stucco	72						
73	A Picket Fence	73						
74	Driveway and Patio	74						
	King's							
75	The One in My Town	75						
76	To Stand Forever	76						
77	Some Things Need Not Change	77						
	The Champion							
78	The Champion: Persistence	78						
79	The Champion: Determination	79						
80	The Champion: Practice	80						
81	The Champion: Demonstrated Ability	81						
	The Young Folks							
82	The Young Folks	82						
83	A Bad Connection	83						
84	The Big Purchase	84						
85	And Now There Are Five	85						
	Ghosts							
86	Do You Believe in Ghosts?	86						
87	Ghosts at Night	87						
88	A Ghost Story	88						
89	Noises in the Attic	89						
90	The Mystery Solved	90						

the head as with the hands. Plan mentally to practice in such a way that improvement will be assured in each of your sustained timings. It is a good idea to know that you are *practicing something* whenever you are typing. Unfortunately, if you aren't sure that you are practicing correct typing techniques, you are probably practicing poor techniques that contribute nothing to your skill but may even detract from it. Guard against wasteful or harmful practice by preplanning each timing and by holding to your plan.

Step 1: Relax
The first step is to relax your shoulders, arms, hands, and fingers. To do this, take a few moments to let your arms hang quietly at the sides of your body. When your arms are in this position, the fingers are naturally curved — the precise curve you want to maintain when typing.

Step 2: Posture Check
Start each practice session with a posture check: your feet should be flat on the floor, your back straight and leaning slightly forward, your body centered opposite the J key about 6 to 8 inches from the typewriter, and your hands on the home row. Correct typing posture contributes to speed, accuracy, and endurance in your performance.

Step 3: Preview Practice
Practicing the preview words which precede each of the timed writings will help you to type the selection faster and more accurately. Type the words slowly at first; then, as you acquire a feel for the words, increase your typing speed until you are typing with precision at your best speed.

Step 4: Set a Goal
The third step is to choose and pursue zealously a goal for your practice. Goals for speed, accuracy, and endurance are easy to establish if you keep a record of the number of lines you can type in a minute. Establish a lines-a-minute score (LAM) by simply counting the lines of typing you can produce in 1 minute. When you know your speed in lines a minute, you can set goals for longer timings of 5 or 10 minutes. For example, if you are able to type 5 lines a minute in a 1-minute timing, strive for a goal of 25 lines in a 5-minute timing, or 50 lines in a 10-minute timing. You can establish goals for any number of minutes simply by multiplying the number of minutes you plan to type by your lines-a-minute score (LAM). If you vary the line lengths you use in the timings (40-, 50-, 60-, or 70-space lines), you can set goals for any speed or accuracy range you choose.

Step 5: Use a Plan for Building Skill
The traditional plan for building skill using timed writings has been (1) to take a timed writing, (2) to practice the words that caused trouble, and then (3) to repeat the timed writing. It's a good plan which has helped millions of typists build their skill. *Sustained Timed Writings* contains 90 selections on which you can practice this plan.

Varying Your Routines
A variety of goal-setting and pacing routines may also be useful in your practice sessions with *Sustained Timed Writings*. The authors suggest several routines that recent studies indicate may help you toward rapid and rewarding self-improvement.

Routine 1: The Pick-a-Speed Plan
If your main objective is speed, this plan is most appropriate.

1. Using the table on the next page, select the words-a-minute speed goal toward which you wish to strive.
2. The number of words you must type to maintain the target speed is indicated for each half-minute interval in the column below your speed goal. In the selection, make an easily erasable pencil mark above the last word you must type at the end of each half-minute interval.
3. Take a series of timings, have your teacher or a "timer" call off each half minute. As you hear the half-minute signals, you know whether you are staying "on target" and, if not, where you are slowing down; and you then know what part of the selection to practice intensively before your next timing.

Routine 2: The Pick-a-Time Plan
When your main objective is *accuracy*, try the pick-a-time routine.

1. From the right side of the table, select the length of time for which you wish to type at a certain speed *without* error or with perhaps not more than *one* error.
2. Now use the chart to determine how many words you must type within the time and at the speed you have chosen. In the selection, make a light pencil mark over the last word you must type, to type with minimum error for the time interval you have selected.
3. Take as many timed writings as are necessary to reach your pick-a-time goal.

Routine 3: The Add-a-Line Plan
Another way to increase speed is the add-a-line plan. After you become familiar with it, you can devise variations to suit your particular needs.

1. Take a 2-minute writing at your normal typing speed, and then count the lines of typing on your paper (fractions of lines count as whole lines).
2. Turn your paper back to the first line of typing. Take another 2-minute writing on the same copy, your goal being to add one more line of typing to the first writing. Type at the fastest rate you can, right over the first writing. This procedure saves paper and frees you of the concern that someone will see any errors you may make. Repeat this step until you do add a whole line.
3. Then take another 2-minute writing at your normal speed, but start at the point in the copy where you stopped in the preceding step. Turn your paper back as before and repeat 2-minute writings until you have added another full line of typed copy.
4. Repeat the steps above until you have practiced the entire timed-writing selection. Then take a 5- or 10-minute writing to check your progress.

Repeat these four steps daily for ten days. You'll be pleased with the improvement you have made!

Routine 4: The Variable-Line Writing Plan
Variable-line writing is another good way to build speed with accuracy.

1. Set the margin stops for a 50-space line, and take a 2-minute writing at your normal rate of speed. Count the number of lines you have typed on your paper.
2. Set the margins for a 60-space line. Take 2-minute writings at your fastest rate until you can type the same number of 60-space lines as you did 50-space lines. When you can do that, set your margins for a 70-space line and repeat 2-minute timings until you can type as many 70-space lines as you did 60-space lines.

About the Timed-Writing Selections

James N. Kimball and A. A. Bowie, both now deceased, wrote the original versions of most of the timed-writing selections used in Sustained Timed Writings. The material

ROBERT L. GRUBBS
JAMES L. WHITE

provides the most effective speed-building materials to help you improve your typing skill.

The Material Has Been Adapted

Of such material are the selections in this book. The present authors have injected the warmth, life, and charm of the original writings into the materials prepared for Sustained Timed Writings. The punctuation, grammar, and language, however, conform to today's writing style. They have adapted the selections to stand alone as 90 separate 5-minute selections; and they have arranged some of the anecdotes to be convertible from independent 5-minute selections to related 10-minute and 15-minute timed-writing selections. Each page — whether it is a 5-minute selection or is part of a convertible, longer selection —

They also knew that the content of the copy was important. They knew that casual stories and casual observations about everyday life were best. The stories were written to be not so interesting that the eyes of the typist would be drawn away to read what happens in the story, yet not so dull that boredom and inattentiveness would set in. They enlivened their writings with twinkling moments, just humorous enough to cause the typist to relax for an instant.

was used widely by typists in training to participate in international typewriting contests. Both men sought to help typists achieve greater speed and accuracy through the special materials they prepared. They filled the copy with streams of balanced-hand words that could be typed rapidly. They avoided sequences of very short words, knowing that the space-bar stroke is not only the easiest but also the slowest. They injected occasional sequences of one-hand words, first involving one hand and then the other, to give the opposite hand a moment to rest. To reduce the number of capitals, they used long sentences; to reduce the number of slow paragraph indentions, they used long paragraphs.

Keep a Record of Your Progress

To help you keep a record of your progress, a speed and accuracy diary has been provided for you on Contents pages ii–iv. Record the results of your first attempt at each timed writing. Then, after you have had an opportunity to practice the material using any of the suggested routines, record the results of your final timing so that you can measure your progress.

3. Set your margins for a 50-space line, and take a 2-minute writing at your normal rate of speed, starting in the copy where you left off in Step 2. Repeat the above steps until you have practiced the entire timed writing selection. Then take a 5- or 10-minute timing to determine the progress you have made.

Routine 5: Variable-Line Writing for Accuracy
When you wish to employ variable-line writing for accuracy, try the following plan:

1. Set your margins for a 70-space line, and take a 1-minute timing at your normal rate of speed. Count the number of lines you have typed on your paper.
2. Reset your margins for a 40-space line. With perfect accuracy as your goal, take 1-minute writings until you can type without error as many 40-space lines as you did 70-space lines in the 1-minute writing.
3. Reset your margins for a 50-space line. Repeat 1-minute timings until you can type without error as many 50-space lines in a minute as you did 70-space lines. When you can do that, reset your margins for a 60-space line and repeat the process. When you have accurately typed the required number of 60-space lines, set the margins for a 70-space line and follow the same routine.
4. Follow the procedures above until you have practiced the entire selection. Then take a 5- or 10-minute timed writing and note your accuracy gains.

If you want to type this fast (WAM)...												
25	30	35	40	45	50	55	60	65	70	75	80	
You must type this many words...												In:
13	15	18	20	23	25	28	30	33	35	38	40	½ min.
25	30	35	40	45	50	55	60	65	70	75	80	1 min.
38	45	53	60	68	75	83	90	98	105	113	120	1½ min.
50	60	70	80	90	100	110	120	130	140	150	160	2 min.
63	75	88	100	113	125	138	150	163	175	188	200	2½ min.
75	90	105	120	135	150	165	180	195	210	225	240	3 min.
88	105	123	140	158	175	193	210	227	245	263	280	3½ min.
100	120	140	160	180	200	220	240	260	280	300	320	4 min.
112	135	158	180	203	225	248	270	293	315	338	360	4½ min.
125	150	175	200	225	250	275	300	325	350	375	400	5 min.

SEPTEMBER DELIGHT

PREVIEW WORDS

September poets brides palm lazy man midday no time to waste live thing noise tired wings well-known June bug flung mantle filmy brown covers sheet night bird "whip poor Will" theme song climbs blue haze wet fog soothing dreary cold bleak wind chilling rain fiery heat express poetry

WORDS

You may talk as you will; but to me, September is the best month of the year. There are many who agree with me. I know it, for they have told me so. It is not, however, the month of which so much has been said and sung by poets. Nor is September the month that brides select. 14 / 28 / 41 / 55 / 57

With poets and brides, June holds the palm. But to a lazy man like me, there seems to be too much work going on at that time. It is the midday hour of the year; and as there is no time to waste, all must be up and doing. There is no live thing that is not busy in June. By day, the air is full of the noise of their labors, and in the night, you will still hear the hum of the tired wings of the well-known June bug. 71 / 84 / 98 / 111 / 126 / 140 / 142

It is not like that in September. The work of the year has been done, and over it all is flung a mantle of filmy brown as one at the end of the day covers things with a sheet to keep them free from dust. When the sun goes down, all is still, save the cry of the night bird that demands that we "whip poor Will." What Will has done to merit it, I do not know, but that is the theme of the night bird song. As the moon climbs high in the sky, it pierces a blue haze that is not like the cold, wet fog of earlier days but is dry and warm and soothing to the senses. There is none of the dreary cold of winter, the bleak wind and chilling rain of spring, or the fiery heat of summer. 156 / 169 / 182 / 196 / 209 / 223 / 236 / 249 / 264 / 278

In all of September, I find a delight which it is not given to me to express in poetry much as I would like to do so. I can only say once more that to me it is the very best month in all of the year. 292 / 305 / 319

| 1 | 2 | 3 | 4 | 5 | 6 | 7 | 8 | 9 | 10 | 11 | 12 | 13 | 14 |

THE MYSTERY SOLVED

PREVIEW WORDS

aunts knocks ceiling finally looked funny really believe noise
minutes decided attic causing everybody stopped hasty exit either
direction beating interesting climbed lanterns follows closely
skirt played spinning wheel treadle thump experience known resting

My aunts and I heard those same six knocks on the ceiling twice again before my parents finally came home. We told them our story, and they looked at us a little funny as though they did not really believe we had heard a noise at all. They sat down in front of the fire, but in just a few minutes all of us heard the ghost again.

That did it. We all decided to make a trip to the attic to see what was causing the noise. Everybody went to the top of the stairs—well, that is, everybody but me. I went up about halfway and stopped there so I could make a hasty exit in either direction if I saw or heard some things I did not like. My heart was beating very fast, you may be sure.

We must have made an interesting sight as we climbed the stairs to the attic. My parents were in front with lanterns, followed next by the two old women holding on to each other, and a small boy with large eyes holding on to a skirt. As the light played over all the kinds of things one finds in an attic, I found myself making up stories about each piece. My father must have been doing the same thing, for after a while he stopped in front of an old spinning wheel. He gave it a half turn, and just as he did, the treadle which was resting on the floor began to thump six times. By the side of the top of the wheel was a big rat hole, and the rats used the wheel as the best means of getting to and from the floor. My parents moved the wheel away from the hole, and from that time to this that ghost has never been known to walk again. This was my first experience with ghosts, and it was a very real one.

| 1 | 2 | 3 | 4 | 5 | 6 | 7 | 8 | 9 | 10 | 11 | 12 | 13 | 14 |

GHOSTS (continued)

THE NIGHT I DIED

PREVIEW WORDS

awake asleep gear thought pieces rigged trunk elephant reason human doubt badly flowers surface narrow strange bother sensation humor myself expected actually guessed rightly friends predicted exactly completely convinced fixed somebody touched shoulder fasten Chicago

Did you ever lie awake at night, not asleep and yet not awake, with your mind all out of gear, trying to keep tabs on all the thoughts which come to you in bits and pieces? It is at such times that you can see your pet cat sitting on a rug before the fire, rigged out in the trunk of an elephant, and see no reason why she should not look like that.

Of course, you have done all these things because you are human. It was like that with me. I was dead—there was no doubt about it—I was dead and did not feel at all badly about it. In my nose there was a smell of flowers; with my feet I felt the nice smooth surface of the narrow house; and when I put my hands over my head, there it was again. Yes, I was dead, and it did not bother me.

On the other hand, it was a new sensation. And then there came to me a grim sort of humor as I felt how hot it was there. I told myself that, at any rate, I had gone to the right place just as I had expected to. Actually, I took a good deal of pride in the fact that I had guessed rightly. Of course, had I been awake, I would have thought that quite a few of my friends had predicted that this was exactly where I would be.

Anyway, there I was completely convinced that I was dead. So I just turned over in my box and was getting fixed all nice and snug to enjoy it when somebody touched my shoulder and said very nicely, "Please fasten your seat belt as we are going to land in Chicago." So I had come to the end of my journey and must get ready to deplane, but the relief I should have felt was going to be a long time coming.

NOISES IN THE ATTIC

PREVIEW WORDS

night ghost walked thirty windows deeply covered scratch panes across shining hues diamond elms planted century shadow twig mysteriously branches forty swinging piece frayed remained summer twist retire kitchen companions fireplace whirl suddenly ceiling thumps tingle

WORDS

It was night, of course, for I have never heard of a real ghost that walked in the bright light of day. It was very cold, about thirty below and still going down. The windows were deeply covered with frost, and I had to scratch a place on one of the panes before I could look out. I could see for half a mile across the snow fields, and the full moon was shining on the snow with all the hues of a very large diamond.

Out in the field, I could see the tall elms which were planted there when the house was built a century ago. The shadow of every twig moved mysteriously as the branches waved in the wind. On one of those trees was a branch about forty feet from the ground, and swinging from the limb was a long piece of frayed rope—all that remained of a swing which had been put there during the summer which had passed. The wind gave the rope an extra twist just then, and it seemed to be a good idea to pull down the shade and retire into the kitchen to get a glass of warm milk.

My only companions this night were two elderly aunts who sat knitting on either side of the great open fireplace. It was warm and pleasant, but now and then an icy blast would come roaring down the chimney and whirl the ashes about. The strange light from the fire and the memory of the rope swinging from the elm tree made me feel a little uneasy.

Suddenly, from the ceiling above came six thumps or knocks or raps: one, two, three, four, five, six—just like that. My hair stood on end and my arms and legs began to tingle. I can tell you, I was very scared. The women stopped knitting, and I do believe all of us stopped breathing.

(continued)

| 1 | 2 | 3 | 4 | 5 | 6 | 7 | 8 | 9 | 10 | 11 | 12 | 13 | 14 |

GHOSTS (continued)

POLLY PILSENER

PREVIEW WORDS

generally speaking birds English language some system exception tongue parrot ambition plenty of proof fixed mind "Polly wants" point beaten express herself understood sometimes ein beer actually beverage Pilsener beer brewed special formula curtains glimmer dawn everybody talk plainer

	WORDS
Generally speaking, birds are not very much interested in the	13
English language, or any other language for that matter, although it is	27
quite possible that they may have some system of language of their	41
own. One bird, however, may well be the exception to the rule. This	55
bird, quite often, is interested in speaking in English or some other	69
useful tongue. This bird is called a parrot, and most parrots will learn	84
to talk.	86
There is one parrot which is just full of ambition to talk, and she	100
gives plenty of proof of it every day of her life. She lives in a cage,	115
and as she has no chance to use her wings, she has fixed her mind	128
on the study of English. She is doing fairly well at it. So far, she has	143
got "Polly wants" down to a point so fine that it cannot be beaten.	157
What it is that she wants, she does not seem to know or at any rate	171
she does not seem to be able to express herself in a way that can be	184
understood. It sounds sometimes as if she says, "Polly wants ein beer."	199
It is really not likely that she is actually calling for the beverage.	214
Because it sounds as though she is, her last name has become Pilsener	228
which as you may know is the name of a type of beer brewed to	240
some special formula.	244
Polly Pilsener loves the language, there is no question about that.	258
Just as soon as the curtains of the night are drawn back from the sky	272
to let in the first glimmer of dawn, that parrot's cage is hung near the	287
window. In less than two minutes, everybody is aware that she wants	301
to have something, but nobody is sure just what it is. But the bird	315
has a lot of ambition. Everybody is sure Polly will talk plainer soon.	329

|1 |2 |3 |4 |5 |6 |7 |8 |9 |10 |11 |12 |13 |14 |

A GHOST STORY

PREVIEW WORDS

ghosts experiences qualify expert subject beginning though recall
details slight ticking clock corner listening intently sounds level
winter ground heaped drifted nothing vast covering except Nature steep
height flight reached attic seldom different window mainly encounter

WORDS

    Let me tell you some of my experiences with ghosts in order that I may qualify as an expert on the subject. I shall begin at the beginning and shall have to go back a good way, for I was but ten years of age when I met my first ghost. The experience made a deep impression on my mind, and even though it was a long time ago, I can recall all of the details. Even so slight a thing as the ticking of the tall clock in the corner of the room comes back to me now, and I can count those ticks just as I sat and counted them while listening intently for other sounds in the house.

    The old house sat back some way from the main road and was only a story and a half in height. It was an old house and the living rooms were all on the first floor with an attic above which was reached by a short flight of steep stairs. I seldom went into the attic, mainly because it was much too big and lonely for a small boy of ten. It was not so bad in the daytime, for there was a window at each end; but at night it was a very different sort of place and I never went up there alone.

    It was winter, and such a winter as you who live in big cities know nothing at all about. Over hill and dale as far as the eye could see, the snow lay five feet deep on the level ground. In many places, it was heaped and drifted into great piles almost as big as the house itself. There was nothing to break that vast covering of white except in those few sunny places the top of a stone wall or fence could be seen. Everywhere else, Nature had put the world to sleep, and it was a perfect time for my first meeting with a ghost. I will not forget it.

(continued)

| 1 | 2 | 3 | 4 | 5 | 6 | 7 | 8 | 9 | 10 | 11 | 12 | 13 | 14 |

GHOSTS *(continued)*

NEVER AGAIN

PREVIEW WORDS

summer house rocky ledge salute blast cannon bored large chunk of iron
welded very loud noise muzzle burst the barrel triple charge of power
pounded sledge trick top of the cliff newspaper corners blowing away
fire paper boom soaring roof toolshed backyard remove "never again"

Years ago, I was at my summer home, as is usual with me in the month of August. My house was near the river but high above it on a rocky ledge. It was a good place to watch the boats go by, and it was my custom to salute them with a blast from a cannon a friend had made for me.

He had bored out a large chunk of iron, and welded up the end so that it made a fairly good gun, at least for making a very loud noise. I had loaded it up to the muzzle many times and had told my friend quite often that I would burst the barrel for him before I quit. He said that it was not in me to do it, and after that, there was but one thing for me to do, and that was to go to it. One day, I put in a triple charge of powder and filled the rest of the barrel with stones and pounded them down with a sledge. I aimed to do the trick this time, but if I did, it was no way my idea to be near it when it went off. So I took it out to the top of the cliff, a little way from my house, and set it up with the end sticking out an inch or so from the edge. Then I took a newspaper and put stones on the corners to keep the wind from blowing it away. On the paper I put a pile of powder over the touch-hole of the old iron cannon. When I had done all this, I set fire to the end of the paper and ran for all I was worth. It was a good thing that I ran.

The old cannon went off with a boom. A big piece of iron went soaring over my house and right through the roof of the little toolshed in the backyard. It took me a month to remove the iron and mend the roof. When it comes to cannons, it is "never again" for me.

GHOSTS AT NIGHT   87

PREVIEW WORDS

because ghost exist friend invited haunted agreed asserted belief never something willing horns hooves tail brave shadows prove theory visit sick eight another direction somehow opinion matter during mystery varnish scorn doubting weird uncanny qualify testimony courts

Just because you have never seen a ghost does not mean that ghosts do not exist and that other people have not seen them. I once knew of a case where a friend of mine was invited to spend the night alone in a house which was said to be haunted. In the daytime he not only agreed to go but also asserted his belief that there never was and never would be a ghost. He even said something about being willing to eat the first one he met, horns, hooves, and tail. That is just how brave he was.

When night came on and the shadows fell, and when the time came for him to prove his theory, he found that he had to go and pay a visit to a sick aunt who lived some eight or ten miles away in another direction. I have found it to be like that with most people. Somehow they do not seem to have the same opinion of the matter at night that they do during the day, though why this should be so has always been a mystery to me.

These are the things which make it hard for the one who has to tell a story about ghosts. The storyteller knows that sticking to the truth and stating the facts as they are will only be to invite scorn. Yet trying to varnish the story and make it pretty so as to fit the ideas of doubting readers will spoil it by giving half-truths—which may be no better than no truth at all.

For that very reason, when one starts to tell a tale that is really wild, weird, and uncanny in its detail, it is a good thing to do as the experts are made to do in the courts—that is, to qualify their remarks and ask that credit be given their testimony based on past experiences.

(continued)

GHOSTS *(continued)*

THE SINGING FROGS

PREVIEW WORDS

unless older student typewriting chances passing myself looking happy memories thoughts camped edge marshes awake listening tunes frogs choir ducked stretched staring disturb quietly walked jacket eased concert volume sound nature harmony lullaby soothing particular

Unless you are really an older student of typewriting, the chances are quite good that I am much older than you. With the passing of each year, I find myself looking back at so many happy times when I was young. While I know this is a sure sign of old age, such memories make me very happy, and I want to share this story.

The other day, my thoughts ran back to a time when, as a lad, I had camped out in a tent by the edge of some marshes. The night was warm, and I lay awake listening to the tunes sung by the frogs. I do not know any other sound in nature that is half so sweet. Their sounds are all harmony, and I know of no lullaby that is more soothing.

The singing of the frogs on this particular night was louder than I had ever heard. As with most pleasant things, there comes a time when you want to turn down the volume or at least change the tune. So it was that, after a while, I knew that I would not be able to sleep until I paid a visit to the concert hall. I eased out of my tent, put on my shoes and jacket, and walked quietly down to the edge of the water. I did not want to disturb the singers although I did want to see what I could do about the volume. As I drew near to the edge of the marsh, I saw a frog sitting still and looking at me with its staring eyes. It was a big one that looked even bigger as he stretched his head to see what kind of thing I was. We looked at each other for what seemed like a very long time. Then he ducked under the water and swam over to the choir. He spoke to them, and for the rest of the night they were quiet.

DO YOU BELIEVE IN GHOSTS?

PREVIEW WORDS

ghost rather openly knowing inclined shrug shoulders wrinkle brows anything myself reason attitude admit indeed dictionary printed flaw defined spirit demon specter argument discredit bearer because matter center earth either assume logic stomach reason without wink across

This is a ghost story, or rather it is a story about ghosts. Now, I say this openly and above board, knowing so well that there are a great many people who are inclined to shrug their shoulders and wrinkle their brows and wink one eye when they read anything of the kind. So be it.

As for myself, I could never see any good reason for such an attitude, for we must all of us admit that there are ghosts. If there were no ghosts, we would not find the word in the dictionary; and we do find it there printed in type just as big as any word there is. Now, a ghost is defined as a spirit without a body, or a spirit of any kind; a demon, a specter, and things like that. If there were no ghosts, there would be nothing about them in that book, would there? I can see no flaw in that argument; can you? And if there are ghosts, it stands to reason that somebody must run across one now and then.

Now, if somebody runs across a ghost and comes and tells you about it, why should you try to discredit the bearer of such news? Of course there are ghosts, and you have no reason to doubt it just because you have never seen one. For that matter, you have never seen the center of the earth either. But I assume you believe there is a center and that our lives are better off because of it. Using the same logic, one just might as well eat green apples and then claim that there was indeed no such thing as a bad pain in the stomach because one never saw the pain. And it may be that you have never seen a ghost simply because you were sure that you did not ever want to see one as long as you lived.

(continued)

GHOSTS

TOMORROW

PREVIEW WORDS

material school beginning stride present therefore greater importance represents opportunities future uncertain almost tomorrow without fail cannot away night follow whichever corner whenever forward upon always demands heart yesterday accede training past action study looking stay

To none more than to you who are students in school today does the title of this material mean so much. To you, who live in the present and are at that age when you are beginning to take life in its stride, the future means a great deal. It represents your life as it has to be lived, and as you have lived it up to the present time; and it should, therefore, be of much greater importance to you than is the present.

You are concerned with the present only insofar as it represents your opportunities for the future. You may be uncertain of almost all things in your life; but of one thing you can and must always be sure, and that is that tomorrow without fail always comes. This is one of the facts from which you cannot get away. It is as true as that night must follow day, or day must follow night.

The future is just around the corner; and whenever it comes upon you, that future, to which you have been looking forward, will not stay to inquire whether you are prepared for it. It will surely come with its challenge and its demands; and, if you have worked well, with mind and with heart, in the present, which is now, this very day, but which in the future will be yesterday, you will be able to take up that challenge and accede to those demands. You will be able to make good; it is sure.

It is a matter of training for the future. We may learn much from a study of the past, but we must know in a very real way that it is in the future that all the action will take place. If you stop to think about your own future, today is the first day of the rest of your life.

AND NOW THERE ARE FIVE

85

PREVIEW WORDS

proper ways good business newcomer consumated on the spot transfer cash restaurant table kitchen coffee overjoyed purchase pride in ownership heart and mind clean and spruce kitchen realized enthusiasm take hold together best good in town discovered register young quick afraid five

WORDS

Surely there may be other proper ways to get into the food business, and if you are ever of such a mind, it would be wise to think of some of them. But as you might guess, Jack, the newcomer to our town, just agreed to buy and the deal was consumated on the spot. There had been a meeting of the minds and a transfer of cash to make it binding. Jack had bought a restaurant and was now taking his wife to see the shop.

Jack and his bride entered the little restaurant. They sat down at a table, and then Jack went into the kitchen to get her a cup of his famous coffee. It would not be fair to tell you that the gentle wife was at this moment overjoyed with the purchase, but the longer she sat at the table the more the feeling of pride in ownership began to fill her heart and mind. When Jack returned with the coffee and sat down beside her, they started to talk about the place. He explained how he would first of all clean and spruce up the whole restaurant— kitchen and dining room. Yes, that was the first thing he would do. Of course, the coffee would always be as good as he had just made and brought her, and he would serve food just as good. Yes, she realized that the coffee was good, and his enthusiasm was beginning to take hold of her. Together, they would build a fine business serving the best food in our town.

There was a lot to learn. They quickly discovered that they had to be in the dining room, in the kitchen, and behind the cash register all at the same time. But they were young and quick and not afraid to work, as you can tell when visiting any of the five shops they own.

| 1 | 2 | 3 | 4 | 5 | 6 | 7 | 8 | 9 | 10 | 11 | 12 | 13 | 14 |

THE YOUNG FOLKS (continued)

MY FOREBEAR, THE TEACHER

PREVIEW WORDS

exact three hundred fifty England landed village Boston conditions actually offered educated master languages president Harvard talents according ability position fifty dollars lucky managed thrown salary grandfather descendants followed famous forebear Henry Dunster example

	WORDS
A long time ago, or to be a little more exact, it was something	13
like three hundred fifty years ago, a man came over from England and	27
landed at the then little village of Boston. He was doing just what you	42
and I would have done under the same conditions: he was looking for	56
a job.	58
Actually, he had been offered a job, and now he had come over	71
here to take it, if he liked what he saw. He was an educated man for	85
his day, for he was a master of many languages and had been a	97
teacher in his old home. That was the sort of job he had been offered	112
in this country—that of head teacher, later called president of Harvard.	127
If it is true that people are always paid according to their talents,	142
one might think very little of the ability of the first president of	155
Harvard. His salary after he had held the position for eight or ten	169
years was only one hundred fifty dollars a year; and often it was by	183
some lucky chance that he managed to get any of it at all. In fact,	197
for two years, he got nothing. And there was a hundred dollars still	211
owing to him when he was thrown out, or fired, or removed—any way	224
you may choose to put it, the end result still being the same.	237
This man was my grandfather, if you put about six greats before	250
the word. He was a teacher, and a good many of his descendants have	264
also followed the path he made and become teachers of one thing or	278
another. While none of us ever became president of a famous school	291
like Harvard, most of us have been lucky enough to hold on to our	304
teaching jobs and enjoy a good life. My forebear, Henry Dunster, set	318
a good example.	322

| 1 | 2 | 3 | 4 | 5 | 6 | 7 | 8 | 9 | 10 | 11 | 12 | 13 | 14 |

THE BIG PURCHASE 84

PREVIEW WORDS

to happen next high in the heavens promising sort work evidently nothing pleased with himself face beamed restaurant over on Wood Street gentle surmised small savings breakfast coffee was the worst owner angry knew kitchen had to admit much better discussing many things sell business

WORDS

Well, you just never know what is going to happen next, and that	14	661
was certainly the case for Jack and his new bride who had just arrived	28	675
in our town. Before the sun was very high in the heavens, Jack had	42	689
gone into the city to see if he could find a promising sort of work	55	702
to do. While he was gone, the young wife was thinking what she	68	715
might do. But even as she was giving the matter her thought, friend	82	729
husband came back. Now what is wrong, she wondered. Evidently	95	742
nothing, for he seemed very pleased with himself, and his face beamed	109	756
with happiness. "We own a restaurant. I bought one this morning over	123	770
on Wood Street."	127	774
This does not make sense, the gentle bride thought, although she	141	788
was very careful not to say anything like that to Jack. First of all, he	155	802
turns down a job about which he knows something, and the next day,	169	816
he is in a business about which he knows nothing. And she surmised	182	829
that their small savings had gone into the purchase of the shop. She	196	843
was right. Jack assured her, however, that everything was all right.	211	858
He explained how the deal came about. While having breakfast in	225	872
this little shop, Jack had told the owner that the coffee was the worst	239	886
that he had ever tasted and that he could make better coffee himself.	253	900
The owner got angry and said that if he knew so much about coffee,	267	914
he had better go out into the kitchen and make it himself. And this	280	927
is what Jack did. The owner had to admit that Jack's coffee was much	294	941
better. They fell to discussing many things, and the owner said that	308	955
he really wanted to sell the business. Jack said that he would like to	323	970
buy it.	325	972

(continued)

| 1 | 2 | 3 | 4 | 5 | 6 | 7 | 8 | 9 | 10 | 11 | 12 | 13 | 14 |

THE YOUNG FOLKS (continued)

IN GRANDFATHER'S TIME

PREVIEW WORDS

grandfather story teller recall wishing getting hectic painted
July Sunday humid warmth country through window church perfumes
violet pleasing quiet melody nature brook rippled danced pebbly
blossoms peaceful cemetery worship farmers together moss-covered

When I was a boy, my grandfather used to tell me about life in the old days. He was such a good storyteller that I recall wishing that I could have lived in his time, too. Now that I am getting older and life is getting more hectic, the scene he painted is even more dear.

"It was the end of July and the day was hot—not with the close and humid warmth of the great city, for it is not like that in the country. The air was warm and dry on that Sunday as it came through the open window of the church. Every tiny puff of air was filled with the odor of pine and fir, of wild rose and violet, and all those other perfumes of the woods which are pleasing to the nose and also to the being.

"And it was not just the air that made one feel at peace with the world, but it was also the quiet of all about you. The air was full of the melody of nature, of the sound of the cool little brook as it rippled and danced over its pebbly bed just outside the door. There was the low hum of the bees as they stole the sweets from the clover blossoms. There were the lovely songs of the birds which year after year built their nests and raised their young in the trees that hung over the moss-covered stones in the peaceful church cemetery.

"The day and the air and the woods and the church all came together for a perfect day of rest and peace. The work in the fields was done for one more week, and the farmers for many miles about had come here to worship in their own way. It was a time and a place to put all the cares of the world out of your mind and be at peace with yourself."

| 1 | 2 | 3 | 4 | 5 | 6 | 7 | 8 | 9 | 10 | 11 | 12 | 13 | 14 |

A BAD CONNECTION

PREVIEW WORDS

very hopeful local mail order house interview much worried quiet voice company officials small savings think over the matter this big company pretty bad shape Jack pessimistic about situation discouraged failure avoided connection refreshed confident sun casting first rays breakfast

The nice young man and his bride who had come to our town were very hopeful that he would land a good job at the local mail order house. When he returned so quickly from his interview to their hotel, the bride was much worried. But she merely asked him, in a quiet voice, what had happened at the interview. He told her everything that had taken place.

Almost the first thing that the company officials wanted to know was how much money he could invest. When he told them of his small savings, they said that the amount would not be enough. So he said that he would like to think over the matter. On his way back to the hotel, he thought this way: If this big company was interested in his small change, they must be in pretty bad shape, and he would be better off if he got a job in some other place. So that is what he decided to do.

Jack—that is what his friends called him—did not seem pessimistic about the situation nor was he discouraged by his failure to land this particular job. If anything, he looked relieved that he had avoided the connection. He proposed that they eat and retire early so that he could get a good night's rest and be refreshed to start out in the morning. He was confident that he could find something to do very soon.

The next morning he was up bright and early and left the hotel just as the sun was casting its first rays on the river. He did not stop to order his breakfast, such was his hurry. This latter piece of information is important, because if Jack has paused for breakfast at the hotel dining room, his whole life might have been quite different.

(continued)

THE YOUNG FOLKS *(continued)*

THE LEGEND OF ST. NICK

PREVIEW WORDS

cartoonist gentleman Santa Claus pictured white-bearded clothed ermine legend St. Nicholas Dutch settlers church New Amsterdam honor bishop Myra Asia Minor century earliest manifested miraculous daughters purses miracles merchants insignia moneylenders pawnbrokers reindeer sleighs

	WORDS
It is said that a cartoonist named Thomas Nast made the first	13
picture of the old gentleman we know as Santa Claus. Nast pictured	27
Santa as a white-bearded, heavy, older man clothed in red with ermine	41
trim. But the story of Santa goes way back in time, long before Mr.	54
Nast.	56
The legend of St. Nicholas, or St. Nick, was brought to America	69
by early Dutch settlers who named their first church in New Amsterdam	83
in his honor. St. Nicholas was a bishop of Myra, in Asia Minor, during	98
the fourth century, and in his earliest childhood he is said to have	112
manifested miraculous holiness. Hearing of a poor man who planned	125
to sell his three daughters into slavery because he had no dowry for	139
them, young Nicholas dropped three purses of gold into their window,	153
enabling the girls to marry. Tales of miracles worked for sailors at sea	167
led merchants to adopt him as their patron. The purses, or three golden	182
balls, became their coat of arms. Later, the three golden balls became	196
the insignia of moneylenders, or as we know them, pawnbrokers. Soon,	210
St. Nicholas became the patron of children, maidens, mariners, scholars,	225
and bankers—as well as pawnbrokers—literally all over the world.	229
Nearly seven hundred years later, Nicholas became the patron saint	243
of Russia, and his fame spread to the Lapps, the people of the reindeer	257
sleighs. The Lapps probably inspired the stories of St. Nick's reindeer	272
and his home and huge toy factory in the bitter cold, far North. Thus,	286
St. Nick has been symbolized as the jolly bestower of gifts to children.	301
And Rudolph, the red-nosed reindeer, has become as famous as St.	314
Nick.	316

| 1 | 2 | 3 | 4 | 5 | 6 | 7 | 8 | 9 | 10 | 11 | 12 | 13 | 14 |

THE YOUNG FOLKS

PREVIEW WORDS

afternoon winter South Side Station December bride collar worn possibly walked from the station smaller hotels young dressed city streets heavy slush snowing and raining hailed a cab center of the city mail order house promising for advancement necessary reservations later so quickly

WORDS

One afternoon in winter, a long, long time ago, a train arrived in	14
our town. That of itself is not news. It was not then, and it would	28
not be today. But on that train that drew into the South Side Station	43
on that December afternoon was a certain man and his bride. The story	57
goes that this youth, for he was no more than that, wore a collar	70
much too big for him; and his suit looked as though it might have	83
been worn many times, possibly by someone other than him. If the	96
young man had been alone, he would have walked from the station,	109
across the bridge over the river to one of the smaller hotels or boarding	124
houses, put up for the night, and gone about his way as many others	138
were doing at that time.	143
But he had a young bride with him, and she was dressed in her	156
very best. The city streets were heavy with slush, for it had been	170
snowing and raining. Instead of walking the city streets, he hailed a	184
cab and ordered the driver to take them to a hotel in the center of	198
the city.	200
The couple had come to our good town because the young man	213
had been offered a position in a mail order house that seemed more	226
promising for advancement than the job he had held in the general	239
store in a little town rather a good distance away. After reaching the	254
hotel and making the necessary reservations, he left his young bride	268
while he set out to see about the new job. In all too short a time,	281
it seemed to her, he returned. She had expected that he would be	295
taken on at once and, therefore, would not be back until much later	308
in the evening. Why had he returned so quickly to the hotel?	321

(continued)

| 1 | 2 | 3 | 4 | 5 | 6 | 7 | 8 | 9 | 10 | 11 | 12 | 13 | 14 |

DESIRE

PREVIEW WORDS

wrong opinion human another career torment burning desire somebody owner indeed believe seldom moment ordinary longing covets plainly difference easily obtained prone riper juicy fruit hangs fairly grasp remember dreaming certainly friends speeding envy achieve leaving

	WORDS
Of course, I may be wrong; but I am of the opinion that there are	14
no human beings who have not, at one time or another in their careers,	28
been kept awake at night by the torment of some burning desire. The	42
desire may be to do the thing which they know somebody else has	55
been able to do or to become the owner of a thing the likes of which	68
they have seen someone else have. Indeed, I will go so far as to say	82
that I believe that there is seldom a moment in the life of the ordinary	97
person when deep down there may not be found a longing of that	109
sort.	111
It may be that one often covets a thing which is plainly out of	124
reach, but that makes no difference. In fact, it may only serve to make	139
the longing more acute. Then again, there are times when the object	153
we want can be easily obtained, in which case the ease with which	166
it may be had causes it to lose much of its value in our eyes. As a	180
rule, we are prone to set a very high price on that which is out of	193
our reach, just as the fruit at the top of the tree seems riper and	207
more juicy than that which hangs lower down and is fairly within our	221
grasp.	222
Do you remember your longing and dreaming about your first car?	236
I certainly do. For a long time, I saw first one and then another of	250
my friends get into a car and go speeding away, leaving me to wonder	263
if I would ever own one myself. I did not really envy them their cars.	278
It was just that I wanted to have one of my own that I could enjoy	291
and that I could share with my friends. My desire to have a car made	304
all those years of work and saving worthwhile to achieve this ambition.	319

|1 |2 |3 |4 |5 |6 |7 |8 |9 |10 |11 |12 |13 |14 |

THE CHAMPION: DEMONSTRATED ABILITY

PREVIEW WORDS

concentrated effort responsible shorthand contests popular at that time demonstrated ability turning point address Governor nominated Presidency transcript admiration stenographer experiences foreign democratic king stickpin gold cigar presents interesting human dramas players affairs

The days and nights of concentrated effort were no doubt responsible for the very fine work that our young man did in the shorthand contests, which were so popular at that time, and in the important positions that he later attained. His demonstrated ability was a main reason for his being chosen to report a speech that was a turning point in his life.

While still a young fellow, he was sent to report an address of the Governor of New Jersey. He did so well that when this Governor was nominated for the Presidency of the United States, he sent for the young lad whose accurate transcript had won his admiration. At the close of the campaign, the lad returned to his job as a stenographer.

He was later called to serve as personal stenographer and official reporter to the newly elected President. It was with the President that he went to Europe and had the unique experience of living in the palace of a king, for it surely was unique for a commoner to live with royalty.

This young man lived a long and exciting life with travels throughout the world. He told many interesting stories of his experiences in all of the foreign lands he was privileged to visit while in the service of the President. One democratic king presented him with a very beautiful stickpin, and a gold cigar case was given to him by another. But of such presents he rarely talked. He told only of the interesting human dramas and of the players in the affairs of the world.

These things are important, but it should be remembered only that it was his mastery of shorthand that led to his success.

THE CHAMPION *(continued)*

TO SOLVE A PROBLEM

PREVIEW WORDS

material years research purchasing department developing ideas applied efficiency in industry laboratories lifetimes discovery searching very maintain progress nation abundance lacked projects country far advanced technology invention devices consistent create different products which

What we buy is not just so much material that we can see; it is often the result of years of research. Everyone knows that research is very important in modern industry. We like to think of the research department as a place that deals with new ideas, a purchasing department for developing ideas that can be applied with efficiency.

What the workers in our research laboratories are trying to do is to solve a problem. The problem, in broad, general terms, most often is the problem of finding out what we shall do when we cannot keep on doing what we are doing now. What comes next in our lifetimes will be based upon our discovery of what can be done. Through research, we are not only improving the products that we make now, but we are searching for new ones. This is a very important matter, which I am sure you must know; for it is only through new products that we maintain progress.

For years, we as a nation have had an abundance of people, money, and materials. From time to time, we have lacked enough projects to put them all to work; and it is often said the country is too far advanced in technology and that technology will put people out of jobs. This theory is based on the mistaken idea that our research has to do only with the invention of devices to save labor. Nothing could be further from the truth. The greatest goals of research are those consistent with finding devices to create more and different products which will, in turn, create more jobs, more income, and a better climate for living for more people. Through research we live longer and better than ever.

THE CHAMPION: PRACTICE

PREVIEW WORDS

entered phonograph dictating glued recorder flew concentration entrance
impression shortly rapidly judges jury charge court testimony whichever
particular occasions routine local movie silent films ends conversation
explanation flashed screen syllable vocabulary dictionary responsible

WORDS

Every evening after our young friend went to work for the inventor	14	660
of the shorthand system, you could see the light in his office. If you	29	675
entered, you would hear a record playing on his phonograph, dictating	43	689
words, phrases, or straight matter at a rapid rate of speed; you would	57	703
see a young man with his ears glued to the recorder and eyes glued	70	716
to the paper as his hand flew without effort over the paper. His	84	730
concentration was so complete that your entrance would probably have	97	743
made little or no impression upon him.	105	751
But shortly, he would spot you; and if you were one who could	119	765
read rapidly, you would be called upon to dictate a few takes on	132	778
some speech material, a judge's jury charge, or a bit of court testimony—	147	793
whichever he was working on at that particular time or that particular	161	807
evening.	163	809
There were occasions, of course, when he would break from routine	177	823
and go to the local movie. He was a movie fan from the very first,	191	837
and even in those days of silent films, he made them serve his ends.	205	851
When conversation or explanation was flashed on the screen, when	218	864
words of more than one syllable were displayed with which he was	231	877
not familiar, it was for him an opportunity not to be missed. With	244	890
pencil and paper he would make notes and the next day look up new	257	903
words in the dictionary. Then he would assign a shorthand outline for	272	918
them—there was no shorthand dictionary in those days—and make them	285	931
part of his oral and shorthand vocabulary. The days and evenings, even	300	946
those that he spent at the movies, were responsible for the fine progress	315	961
he made.	317	963

(continued)

| 1 | 2 | 3 | 4 | 5 | 6 | 7 | 8 | 9 | 10 | 11 | 12 | 13 | 14 |

THE CHAMPION (continued)

THE DIFFERENCE—ABOUT TWENTY YEARS

PREVIEW WORDS

time and again   industrial research   colleges and universities   country
pure science   applied   twenty   academic   general principles   working   specific
disregard   solution   fisherman   project   national   attention   sounds   simply
study   rub together   friction   very critical   sometimes   enormous   determining

   The question has been asked time and again as to whether there is any difference between what is called industrial research and the research that is being carried on in the great colleges and universities of this country and others. Someone once said that the only difference between pure science and applied science is about twenty years. In other words, those in academic research are working on general principles while in industrial research they are working on specific problems they have.

   In many instances it is necessary to disregard a general solution in order to develop a specific one. It is a good deal like studying the general classes of fish, the different phases in the life of a fish, and the location in which fish are found in order to fish for a living. It is interesting to have this general information, but all the person who fishes wants to know is where the fish are to be found. It does not mean that you are going to catch any more fish than somebody else if you know those other things that the other person does not know.

   A project that continues to hold our national attention sounds very simple. It is the study of why our hands get warm when we rub them together. This occurrence may be easily explained, of course, by saying that the cause is friction. We know that friction is good in some cases but bad in others. We can argue about it forever, but that is really almost all we know about friction. But the importance of knowing how to deal with it is very critical because the sometimes enormous force of friction is a determining factor in mechanical devices of virtually all types.

THE CHAMPION: DETERMINATION

PREVIEW WORDS

striving practicing no bones about it social suspended mastering subject vehicle exclusively knowledge English language elementary school and his vocabulary greatly expanding meanings familiar articles newly acquired determination accomplish principal inventor best writers outcome expert

WORDS

When this young man, of whom we are writing, was striving to	13	337
take shorthand rapidly at school, he was doing a better job of it than	27	351
most of the other students. He was spending more time practicing, and	42	366
this led to success. He was attending school to learn shorthand, to	55	379
master it quickly and to learn to write it rapidly. He made no bones	69	393
about it—social activities had to be suspended for the moment. While	84	408
he was mastering this subject that was to serve as a vehicle for him	97	421
to obtain a good living from this world, he was sure that his time	111	435
should be given over exclusively to the one subject that would open	124	448
the way for him.	128	452
His knowledge of the English language was no better than that of	142	466
an elementary school graduate, and his vocabulary was small. He knew	156	480
it and knew what to do to improve this condition. He found that his	170	494
study of shorthand was greatly expanding his knowledge of English. He	184	508
would look up the meanings of all words that he came across with	197	521
which he was not familiar. Always, he kept a file of cards on which	211	535
he wrote the new words and their meanings. He would write sentences	225	549
and articles, using as many of these newly acquired words as he	237	561
possibly could.	241	565
The determination to accomplish what he set out to do brought	254	578
our friend to the attention of the principal of the school, and through	269	593
him it was made possible for the young fellow to meet the inventor	282	606
of the system of shorthand he wrote. The inventor was, of course,	295	619
particularly interested in finding the best writers of his system. The	310	634
outcome of the meeting was a job in the inventor's office.	322	646

(continued)

| 1 | 2 | 3 | 4 | 5 | 6 | 7 | 8 | 9 | 10 | 11 | 12 | 13 | 14 |

THE CHAMPION (continued)

RABBITS AND COYOTES

PREVIEW WORDS

perhaps common animals jackass rabbit resemblance namesake reality concerned enemy discover believes sagebrush deduce coyote latter streak lightning family traditions tribe coward anything sneaking mesquite unwary usually abundant bounty disappear scenery interesting

Perhaps the most common of all the animals to be found in the cactus country is the jackass rabbit, called by that name because of a sort of resemblance to its namesake. In reality, that only goes as far as the ears are concerned, for they are very long when the animal is sitting up on the lookout for an enemy. You can often discover their owner when he believes that he is safely hidden behind a bit of sagebrush, for you can see the ears and deduce the fact that where there are ears, very long ears, there must also a rabbit be.

The soft-footed coyote hunts the rabbit, and if he is able to catch the rabbit asleep, he makes a meal out of him. However, if the rabbit sees his enemy first, the latter simply knows he is out of luck and turns back and says things that would not look pretty in print, I suppose. At any rate, he knows it is of no use to chase that streak of lightning.

The coyote is a sort of wolf, or at least he is a member of the wolf family. Yet, he does not live up to the traditions of the tribe for he is a coward and never bets on anything except a sure thing. I have seen him many times sneaking through the mesquite in search of some unwary bird or rabbit. His hide is usually bare in spots due to an abundant crop of fleas. But he is not proud, so his appearance does not seem to bother him. He is often seen alone, though sometimes he hunts in packs. His hide is worth more than that of other desert animals for there is a bounty upon it. I shall be sorry to see him disappear, but only because he is an interesting part of the scenery in the desert.

THE CHAMPION: PERSISTENCE

78

PREVIEW WORDS

study shorthand commenced work stenography fifteen factory so engaged fourteenth birthday take dictation typewriter necessity augment income hard day's work ability stick fast objective accomplished achievement attain distinction champion ambition succession dominant persistence

	WORDS
How old were you when you started the study of shorthand if	13
indeed you have commenced your work in this subject? One man who	26
was to become very well known in the field of stenography began the	40
study of shorthand when he was fifteen years of age. He had been	53
working in a factory office at the time and had been so engaged since	67
his fourteenth birthday. He realized that more money could be earned	81
if he were able to take dictation from the manager and transcribe it	95
on the typewriter, and there was an urgent necessity that he augment	109
the family income. He could not leave his job to learn shorthand,	122
however, so he took up the study at night in a business school in a	136
nearby town.	138
It was a long ride to and from school after a hard day's work, but	153
he made up his mind that it was worth the effort, and he held to it.	167
Perhaps it was the ability to stick fast, to hold on till the objective	181
was accomplished, that led him to success in the shorthand field.	195
Maybe it had something to do with the achievement of one of his	207
boyhood goals, to become the fastest shorthand writer in the world,	221
because as is shown by the record, he did attain that distinction. It	235
may have helped him as he strived to become the champion shorthand	249
writer of the world, an ambition he attained two years in succession,	263
as the published reports of the national association under which the	276
contests were conducted will show. It may have been the dominant	290
factor in taking him to the White House, where he served as personal	303
stenographer and official reporter to the President of the United States.	318
His persistence was evident.	324

(continued)

| 1 | 2 | 3 | 4 | 5 | 6 | 7 | 8 | 9 | 10 | 11 | 12 | 13 | 14 |

A POTATO RACE

PREVIEW WORDS

potato exciting sport points start fresh placed runner signal common contestant looking question instance ground farther forward faster theory beyond thinking decided wise calf seemed easier getting heavier result perfectly natural grown ox trouble moral learning therein type

	WORDS
Did you ever see a potato race? It is run in the open air and it	14
is not a very exciting sport. Yet it has its good points all the same,	28
and one of them is that you have to start all over again every time	42
you add a fresh potato to your pile. This is the way the race is run.	56
All who are in it stand at the same starting point. The potatoes	70
are placed eight or ten yards in front of each runner. At a given	83
signal, each contestant starts for the first potato, grabs it, brings it back,	99
and starts over again. You may only bring back one potato on each	112
trip.	114
Not much of a race you say? Well, that may be so; but it will	127
bear looking into a bit, for it has things in common with the typing	141
speed question that is facing you. For instance, you have to go over	155
the same ground every time you add a potato to your pile, and each	168
time you go a little farther to get the next potato. That is really the	183
way to get a new speed in typing. You take one step forward and	196
then go back and go over all the steps you have taken before, each	209
time a little faster.	214
This same theory comes down to us in an old story about the	227
man who tried to lift an ox but found the job to be beyond his	239
strength. After thinking about it for a while, he decided it would be	253
wise to practice lifting a small calf. He lifted the calf each day and	268
it seemed easier and easier each time. Of course, the calf was getting	282
larger and even heavier; but the man did not even notice that. The	296
result was perfectly natural that when the calf had grown to be an ox,	310
the man had no trouble lifting him at all. Therein lies a moral.	324

| 1 | 2 | 3 | 4 | 5 | 6 | 7 | 8 | 9 | 10 | 11 | 12 | 13 | 14 |

SOME THINGS NEED NOT CHANGE

PREVIEW WORDS

neat family of the founder London lad of seventeen university degree
pharmacy graduation immensely attached absorbed early traditions never
resisted modern improvements ice cream soda fountain comfort and safety
browse tone old-fashioned ancient chemicals pharmacist prescriptions

It would be neat if I could tell you that King's, the oldest store in my town, remains in the family of the founder, but I cannot do so. The store has had eight owners so far, but the name has never changed. The latest owner of the store was brought to this country from London when he was three years old and became an errand boy when he was a young man of fourteen. He studied at a large university nearby where he received a degree in pharmacy. After graduation, he was employed at the historic drugstore; and when his employer wanted to sell the business, the young man bought the place and became immensely attached to it.

The new owner was absorbed with the early traditions of the store, and he intended that it would never change. He has resisted almost all modern improvements; but he did, some years ago, install an ice cream soda fountain and made a few other changes to insure the comfort and safety of those who browse or shop in the store. He has not changed the tone of the shop, however, and it seems certain that he never will. He has refused to remove the old-fashioned bottles, herbs, and the ancient chemicals that continue to adorn the place. The prosperity of the shop sustains his belief that it is a drugstore, not a department store.

The business is a family affair now as it has been at times before. The daughter of the present owner, also a pharmacist, is now working at the shop. She fills prescriptions and sells all of the remedies with a ready smile and appears very much inclined to maintain the store and all of its traditions as her father has. That is very nice.

KING'S (continued)

THE LOBSTER'S NEW SUIT

PREVIEW WORDS

lobster strange disposition naturally always scrap because habit claws finger nippers possible business careful interesting backward forward bite-size feelers weapon swift retreat bottom seaweed provide complete armor shell assumes royal himself advantage defend young slimy another

WORDS

 The lobster is a strange chap, taken all in all. Where he got his disposition, I do not know; but it is the kind that one does not take to naturally for he is always ready for a scrap. Maybe it is because when he is young he has to fight for his life every minute of the day and it has become a habit with him.

 All I know is that all you have to do is point your finger at him and his nippers are up and ready for action. If he once gets hold of you, he hangs on as long as possible; and the part of you that he gets hold of is likely to be out of business for some little time. Because he is so fast, you would be wise to be very careful at all times.

 The lobster is interesting to watch as he swims backward and forward using his big claws to good advantage. These claws come in handy when he needs to defend himself, and he also uses them to tear his food into bite-size pieces. The two long feelers at the tip of his nose help him find his food, and a flip of his tail serves as a weapon and as an aid to making a swift retreat just in case he needs to get away in a hurry.

 The lobster lives on the bottom of the sea among the rocks and slimy seaweed. The rocks and seaweed provide him with a safe hiding place, for he has to hide now and then while he builds a new suit for himself. You see, nature provides him with a complete suit of armor to protect him from his foes. When he gets too big for his armor, he sheds it and then he must hide until he grows another shell. With the new shell, he returns to the open sea and once again assumes his royal role as king.

| 1 | 2 | 3 | 4 | 5 | 6 | 7 | 8 | 9 | 10 | 11 | 12 | 13 | 14 |

TO STAND FOREVER

PREVIEW WORDS

museum don't suppose inquiring historian fragrant mystery crammed full barks of trees prescriptions curled yellow downstairs shelves ancient bottles medicine chests mariner and sailor local residents congested uptown frigates replenished gunboats harbor Roughriders ravages malaria

King's old drugstore is not a museum, and I don't suppose the oldest store in your town is either, but the old shop has enough of the unusual to interest the inquiring historian. If you walk up the worn stairs at the back of the sales floor, you will enter a room filled with fragrant mystery. Around the room are drawers crammed full of leaves, roots, and barks of trees that had their place in the medicine of years ago but which are rarely used today. There are also, in this room, huge piles of old prescriptions on papers that are curled and yellow with age. Downstairs, in the back of the shop, you will find a room lined with shelves that are filled row after row with ancient bottles that held the drugs for the medicine chests of sailing ships long since gone to rest.

For years this store was a favorite of the mariner and sailor; and as wars took place and the soldiers and sailors sailed from this port, they would stock up with the medicines and herbs of this store. The local residents began to move away after some years, to less congested areas uptown, and the store depended upon the sailor trade for its life.

In 1806 sailors from the United States frigates replenished their medicine chests at the shop. Those from gunboats in the struggle between the states also stopped to have their prescriptions filled while their ships were tied up in the harbor. The Roughriders on their return from Cuba came in to purchase medicine to combat the ravages of malaria. Once a whole block adjoining the store was burned out by fire, but the store was not touched. It appears it was destined to stand forever.

(continued)

KING'S *(continued)*

DOWN THE RIVER OF TIME

PREVIEW WORDS

rapidly flowing rowing stream enjoyed peaceful scene longed notice glance
looking another direction certainly recommend driving sights unturned
bound behind beyond shore future really trust oars slowly toward fifty
western memory eternity century vividly yesterday believe marking port

Did you ever stand on the bank of a rapidly flowing river and watch someone rowing a boat down the stream? I have enjoyed such a peaceful scene many times; and I have always longed to be in the boat, too.

The other day, I saw a man rowing down the stream, and yet I could not help notice that he was looking in another direction. At first glance, this did not seem to be a very safe thing to do, and I certainly do not recommend it when you are driving a car. While this gave him a chance to enjoy the sights on both sides of the stream, what lay ahead of him was like the unturned pages of an open book.

It seems to me that I am very much like such a man. I am rowing down the stream of time, and my boat is always on the move, but I do not know what port I am bound for. I can look back over the water behind me, and I can note all that takes place on the shore as the boat moves on. But of what lies beyond, what the future will bring me, I do not really know. I will know about it some day; but until then, I will keep on rowing and trust my skill with the oars will bring me to a safe port in the end.

As the sun goes slowly down toward the top of the western hills, I can look back and see more than fifty miles of the river of life, every mile marking a year. Every year is full of the memory of the things which have been and are now past. No doubt, fifty years seems like an eternity to most of you. But the time will come when the events which took place a half century before will stand out as vividly in your mind as though they were the things of yesterday.

THE ONE IN MY TOWN

75

PREVIEW WORDS

oldest store whole city grandmothers grandfathers relate drugstore King's early days section Fourth Avenue fashionable trading center continues square hitching posts squire coachman carriage good old dobbin safely places or refreshment drays tied up seven seas two-story skyscrapers

WORDS

I am sure there is one in your town wherever you may live. There	14
surely is one in my home town; and to end the suspense, I am	26
thinking about the oldest store in the whole of the city. The fine	40
grandmothers and grandfathers who were born here tell that a drugstore	54
called King's is the oldest store in our town. I know of none older.	68
In the early days of this country, when my home town became a	82
town of some importance, the section around Fourth Avenue was a	95
fashionable trading center; and in the middle of the center, Mr. King	109
founded his drugstore. The center was a very busy place then, and so	123
was King's.	125
Around the square at the end of the street were hitching posts to	139
which the squire would hitch his horse and the coachman, having	152
brought the fine lady to shop, would leave the carriage with good old	166
dobbin safely tied up. It is not known to me just where the coachman	180
took himself in the meantime, although it is believed that places of	194
refreshment were round about where one could satisfy his thirst. And	208
nearby, you could see drays tied up while the goods in them were	221
being removed for quick delivery to the stores or being carted away	235
to the docks at the foot of Fourth Avenue to be stowed on ships and	248
taken over the seven seas.	254
Mr. King's drugstore itself is located in a two-story building which	268
today looks very small alongside the skyscrapers that have grown up	282
in the financial district. While the building may appear somewhat	296
dingy, its large beams in the ceiling defy the passage of time. The	309
horses are gone, and the coachmen too; but King's remains.	321

(continued)

| 1 | 2 | 3 | 4 | 5 | 6 | 7 | 8 | 9 | 10 | 11 | 12 | 13 | 14 |

THE FRIENDLY STREAM

17

PREVIEW WORDS

window pleasant valley flowed stream seemed worthy country untold crept quiet through journey lullaby vegetation inviting bygone chaos silently sparingly mists likely purring bathed breeding fowl darted themselves coyote reflected rushes unknown young colored deeper crane distant mists

WORDS

A few days ago, I looked out of the car window upon a very	12
pleasant valley in which flowed a stream so small that it seemed	26
almost not to be worthy of notice. In fact, it was so small that in my	40
part of the country, it would not even be called a stream. For untold	54
ages, that little brook had crept on in its quiet course from the heart	68
of the hills, down through the valley, on its long journey toward the	82
sea. All that time, it sang its lullaby to the birds and gave life and	96
joy to the vegetation which grew sparingly upon its wide, inviting	110
banks.	112
People of a bygone age, whose very name is now unknown to us,	125
came into being out of the chaos of the past. They lived for a short	138
time in that little valley, and then they silently stole away and were	152
lost to the view in the mists of time. Quite likely, early settlers camped	166
by the side of that purring brook and bathed in its cool waters. And	180
on their journey to distant breeding places, the wild fowl stopped by	194
for a moment to swim in its clear pools. Bright colored fish darted to	208
and fro among the stones in its deeper holes. Surely the deer and the	222
coyote saw themselves reflected on its surface as they came to take a	236
drink, and the mud hen and the crane built their nests in the rushes	250
and there raised their young. The stream was a friend to all who came.	264
There are many streams like this one all over our broad land, all	278
so small that one tries in vain to find any trace of them on the map.	292
Even though they are small, they serve well fish and fowl and deer	305
and man. Small streams make big ones, and they are all a part of the	319
sea.	320

| 1 | 2 | 3 | 4 | 5 | 6 | 7 | 8 | 9 | 10 | 11 | 12 | 13 | 14 |

DRIVEWAY AND PATIO

74

PREVIEW WORDS

brass tacks location questions regarding soil treated cellar gas light nearby schools transportation tax rates neighborhood assessments local prevailing dust gases industrial section parcel of land wooded hilltop carefully selected relation surroundings flower garden driveway patio

	WORDS	
When you get to the brass tacks of thinking about it, location of	14	665
the house suggests many questions. For instance, an answer to the	28	679
question regarding the type of soil on which you are to build will be	42	693
needed. Is it necessary to have the soil treated to make sure that your	56	707
cellar is a dry one? How about the gas and light service, about nearby	71	722
schools, transportation, and about tax rates? You will want to know	84	735
something about the neighborhood as to whether or not it is improving.	99	750
Here is something that you perhaps may not have thought about. Will	113	764
there be any assessments for future local improvements? How about the	127	778
prevailing winds? Do they bring dust and gases from the industrial	140	791
section of a town? Funny, too, you may find yourself with a lovely	154	805
parcel of land with a wooded hilltop but with no way of getting to	167	818
the road or street.	172	823
If it happens that you have a lot now, but cannot build for a	185	836
while, then perhaps you should buy some carefully selected trees and	199	850
have them planted, after you have had the soil checked. While the	212	863
trees are growing, you will want to consider the style of the house	226	877
that you are to build. This matter has to be considered in relation to	240	891
the lot and the surroundings. You want to be sure that when the house	254	905
is built the sun pours into the rooms you intend to live in most, that	269	920
fine trees do the job you intended them to do. There is the flower	282	933
garden to be kept in mind, too, and the area that can best be spared	296	947
for driveway and patio.	301	952
Give thought to the inside of the house and say to yourself, "Here	315	966
is where we shall work, study, play, and entertain. This is our home."	330	981

| 1 | 2 | 3 | 4 | 5 | 6 | 7 | 8 | 9 | 10 | 11 | 12 | 13 | 14 |

HOUSE BUILDING (continued)

AS IT WAS IN THE BEGINNING

PREVIEW WORDS

pulpit Parson Goodman flock pleasing oratory studied social scheme political outburst Father children pitiless cruelty mingled thrush flute-like piped forest perched repress doings passions origin sting poverty homely phrase wealth thud eternal beauty echo strife familiar

High up in the pulpit Parson Goodman talked to his flock. His was no effort at pleasing oratory, no deep and studied social scheme, no political outburst. He told only of the great love of the Father for his children and the pitiless and harsh cruelty of man to mankind.

I did not listen, but I heard it all. It came to me as one hears sounds from a long way off, and the words were mingled with the lovely flute-like note of the wood thrush as he piped his joy of living from the top of the tallest pine in the very heart of the forest. Even so, I could not repress a smile as I thought how little that good man who was perched up there in that high pulpit could know of the doings of the great world outside; how little he and his flock could be stirred by the passions which have their origin in the pride of riches or in the sting of poverty. It was a good sermon all the same, and it told in homely phrase the story of the strife and struggle of this life, of the mad rush for power and wealth, the sorrows and trials of the world, and the eternal joy and peace of the world that is yet to come.

At last he shut the heavy book before him with a thud that sent an echo through the church, and the sermon came to an end with these old and by now very familiar words: "As it was in the beginning, is now, and ever shall be, world without end, amen." Then there was silence.

As the good folks left the church, they spoke to one another with a smile on their faces and a song in their hearts. There was a tone in their voices like the beauty and the peace of the world about them.

A PICKET FENCE 73

PREVIEW WORDS

```
building pitfalls prevent carrying wonderful results systematic manner
really know take advantage expert help available assured to your liking
winter dress blanket of snow smoke curling from the chimney that within
cozy hearth insulated losing heat wasting money beautiful picket fence
```

	WORDS

    Do not think that building a house is so hard and so full of pitfalls as to prevent your carrying out the job. Many people have built houses before you with wonderful results. It stands to reason you will be able to do as well as they if you go about it in a systematic manner with the aid of those who really know how to do the many jobs that go into the building of a house. Take advantage of expert help that is available, and you will be more assured of having a house that is to your liking.

    You may have a picture of your house in mind, a house in winter dress with a blanket of snow on the roof and smoke curling up from the chimney showing that within is a cozy hearth. Wait a minute. Are you sure that your plans call for the roof to be insulated so that heat will not pour out and melt the snow away in no time? Such luck would mean that you are losing heat and wasting money. Those beautiful trees that you had in mind may not grow in the particular spot assigned to them, and may not throw their shadows as you had expected, for two reasons. They may be badly set on the lot, or there may not be enough good soil in which to grow them. Maybe you want a picket fence because it reminds you of your old home in the country. You may be denied the pleasure of the picket fence because fences are not permitted in some residential areas.

    In this short space, we cannot go into every detail of building the house nor the equally important matter of where the house can best be located. There are many things to consider, though, which may be vital to you as you proceed to locate a site and go about building.

(continued)

| 1 | 2 | 3 | 4 | 5 | 6 | 7 | 8 | 9 | 10 | 11 | 12 | 13 | 14 |

HOUSE BUILDING *(continued)*

ALL WORK AND NO PLAY . . .

PREVIEW WORDS

```
pride themselves offices minute through program barely enough subway
family person clause stone resting vacation adding beneath likely dull
didn't working although degree ahead prefer always anyone shady crowd
listen sounds morning always chance country peace myself fellow friend
```

There are people who pride themselves on the fact that they never take a day off from work. Every week day of the year, they open their offices on the minute in the morning, go through the whole day as if by program, and turn the key in the door at night with barely enough time to catch the very last subway or train home to be with the family. Every day is like every other day, and they take great pride in it.

I once knew a person like that who left a clause in his will to the effect that the stone over his last resting place should bear the words, "Here lies one who takes his first vacation." When I told this story to a friend of mine, he said he felt like adding beneath it, "and he is likely to be gone a long time." I am glad he didn't do that.

Working all the time really is not my way. Although I like to work well enough, I am not in love with it to such a degree that I allow it to take all of my time. I work hard at what I do, but I always try to plan ahead for my vacation. I much prefer to take some days off while I am alive and not wait until I am dead when, for all I know, I just might have other things to do. At least, there is always that chance.

All work and no play makes anyone dull. I like now and then to get away from the crowd. It is not that I do not love my fellow man; but in a way, I rather like to think of him working hard at his job in the city while I lie on my back under a shady tree and listen to the sounds of the country. For me at least, there is nothing that makes me feel more at peace with myself than a day alone in the open air.

FRAME, BRICK, OR STUCCO

72

PREVIEW WORDS

house yourself family wonderful decision adventure planned best points contain comfort convenience everything acquire clippings collected ideas foundation roof beware stucco cabin country likely averages realities whatever planning worthwhile details occur doubt perhaps until almost

WORDS

So you are going to build a house for yourself and for your family.	15
That is a fine idea. We are sure that you have a most wonderful	28
feeling about it. You have made your decision, and you are all set to	42
start on a great adventure. You have always had in mind that some	55
day you and your family could live in a house that you had planned,	69
one that would have the best points of all of the houses you have	82
ever seen.	85
There are many things that you want this house of yours to contain	99
for your comfort and convenience. There must be room for all kinds	113
of things that will make your living really worthwhile. There must be	127
places for everything that you have or that you will acquire through	141
the years. We suppose you have many clippings that you have collected	155
over the years. In them, you have found ideas that you would like to	169
see made a part of that house of yours. There is little doubt that in	183
your mind you have the house built from the very foundation to the	196
roof; but there are always many details that do not occur to those	210
planning to build until they are almost ready to build.	221
You may want a frame house or a brick house, or perhaps a stucco	235
one, or you may have in mind a log cabin of the modern type in the	249
country. Whatever you want, it is your dream, and you are now	261
planning to make that dream come true. As this will be the one and	275
only house that you are likely to build, if we take the law of averages,	289
it will be well for you to have some help in making the plans to	302
ensure that all of your mental pictures of your dream house become	316
living and happy realities.	322

(continued)

| 1 | 2 | 3 | 4 | 5 | 6 | 7 | 8 | 9 | 10 | 11 | 12 | 13 | 14 |

HOUSE BUILDING

PULL

PREVIEW WORDS

please contrary pull world drive within exert effort ocean against cannot avail limbs ache breath prow pointed direction teeth moment gale ceasing instant swift events frightful ground harder stern spur necessity nicest struggle faithfully toil suffering stroke well-being

You may say what you please to the contrary, but a pull is one of the best things you can find in this old world of ours. Some pulls are good and some not so good; but the best pull of all is that drive that is within all of us which makes us exert our very best effort always.

When you are alone in a boat on the vast ocean of life, when the wind and the tide are both against you, when the waves are high and you really cannot see the shore, then there is one kind of pull and only one that will be of avail. Then you must take a firm grip on the oars of life, dip them deep in the water, and bend your back with every stroke in order to keep going. Though your limbs ache and your breath fails, you must keep the prow of your ship pointed in but one direction—always into the teeth of the gale, without for a moment ceasing your efforts. If you let go of the oars even for an instant, the swift tide of events all about you will bear you back at a frightful speed; and you will have to go over the same ground again if you are to reach your goal.

There is no pull that is harder, but there is none which pays better in the end, for it is made under the stern spur of necessity. One of the nicest things about this kind of pull is the big reward at the end of our struggle. The history books are filled with examples of this kind of pull, and the names of those who did the pulling can be found on the walls of the Hall of Fame. More than that, not only have they who did the pulling been faithfully rewarded, but their toil and suffering have added much to the well-being of all of us.

ENGLISH? THE EASIEST WAY!

71

PREVIEW WORDS

whether charts simple definitions everyday developed useful languages written concerned difficult precise although complex speaking thought easiest moments spare ideas objectively yourself place whether subject crystal faults beginning background information newspapers magazines

	WORDS	
I cannot say whether you have given the matter much thought, but	14	664
as you chart your way through life, simple definitions for everyday	28	678
things tend to be formed. You may have, therefore, developed some	41	691
very useful definition for the subject of languages. To me, language is	56	706
spoken or written thoughts; as far as I am concerned, language is	69	719
English.	71	721
It is not a difficult matter to speak and write in precise English	85	735
although there are those who say that writing the language is more	99	749
complex than speaking it. But I do not think so; in fact, it is my	112	762
thought that the more you write good English the easier speaking	125	775
becomes.	127	777
The easiest way to learn to write is by writing. When you have	141	791
a few moments to spare, write down some of your thoughts on any	154	804
subject on which you have some ideas. After you have done this, try	168	818
to read what you have written objectively. By that I mean try to put	182	832
yourself in the place of the person who may read what you have	194	844
written. See whether you have made your subject crystal clear. One of	209	859
the faults of many beginning writers is that they forget that they have	223	873
a background of information on the subject that the reader does not	237	887
have. Remember to write clearly enough so that one who does not	250	900
know so much about the subject as you will not have to read into	263	913
your work something that is not there in your writing, but is, unfor-	276	926
tunately, only in your mind.	282	932
If you have some difficulty in finding something about which you	296	946
can write, get into the habit of reading newspapers or magazines.	309	959

|1 |2 |3 |4 |5 |6 |7 |8 |9 |10 |11 |12 |13 |14 |

ENGLISH (continued)

READING IS FUN

PREVIEW WORDS

reading sometimes might suffer called mental indigestion living result pleasure success heroes opinions thinking reflection merely echo wrong attack rewarding writing substitute thriller romance adventure stimulus literature civilization generation exasperate librarian relief repress

While it is said that reading will make a full person, sometimes it can make a person too full. You might suffer from what could be called a case of mental indigestion. We all know people who are so in love with books that they find no time for living. They take their pleasure in the success of the heroes in their books. They live their lives kind of secondhand; and their opinions are not the result of thinking and reflection, but a small echo of things they have read.

No, I am not going to attack reading. On the whole, I do think that reading is, in the long run, one of the most rewarding of all pleasures. If this writing is an attack, it is on reading as a substitute for real thinking. Now, do not get me wrong. No one enjoys a thriller any more than I do, and there must be a place for romance and real adventure in literature. We who work in an office or a study or a classroom find that in such books we work off some of our caveman ideas that we must repress as the price we pay for living in civilization. Each generation has its romantic hero, whether it be Robin Hood or Dick Tracy. The nice thing about adventure books is that they are a relief from thinking.

Reading should not be all relief. Sometimes it ought to provide a stimulus. At least a part of our reading should be planned. It can be very worthwhile to spend a little time in planning our reading each day. One type of reader who really does exasperate me is the person who goes into a library and asks the librarian to choose a good book for him to read. Really, part of the fun of reading is choosing your own book.

| 1 | 2 | 3 | 4 | 5 | 6 | 7 | 8 | 9 | 10 | 11 | 12 | 13 | 14 |

ENGLISH? LEARN BY DOING!

PREVIEW WORDS

discovered person something drive being through steps machinery motion perhaps English hearing cannot structure language doing reading parcel mastering difficult classroom thought worry mathematics realize timed typewriter information assigned only misleading universal subject aspect

Long ago it was discovered that a person does not learn to use something by being told about it. Those of you who drive a car know very well that you did not learn to drive it by being told about it. You had to get into a car and go through the steps that set the machinery in motion so that the car would run. Now perhaps you have been trying to learn English by hearing about it. It cannot be done in that way. You must know the structure of the language if you want to use it well, but you must also learn English by doing—by using it, by writing it, by reading it, by making it part and parcel of yourself at all times.

Do you think of mastering English as something that is difficult? Perhaps when you go into the English classroom that thought is in your mind, but it is not a matter about which you should worry. You can and should learn to use proper English in every classroom you enter, even the one for mathematics. If you just stop to think about it, you will realize that you have to use English in schoolwork.

Those of you who are writing this timed copy know that you are using English when you use the typewriter. You have been told this truth by your teacher, no doubt. But I suppose that the fact that you were in a classroom when this information was given to you and that one teacher was assigned to teach you only English may have been misleading to you.

English is a universal subject, and by that I mean that you must use it in every class and in every aspect of your life. Since that is the case, you may master it best as you learned to drive—by doing.

(continued)

| 1 | 2 | 3 | 4 | 5 | 6 | 7 | 8 | 9 | 10 | 11 | 12 | 13 | 14 |

ENGLISH *(continued)*

THE FOURTH DIMENSION

22

PREVIEW WORDS

great believers fourth dimension refer explain quickly important instead considered first designing excite the market manufacturing material and energy pure science customer the cost factor fashion afford to acquire aspects of production packing case consumer skilled labor thousand ideas

    We have always said that we are great believers in what may be called the fourth dimension. You may not know just what is meant when we refer to a fourth dimension in manufacturing so let me explain quickly that the fourth dimension is cost. It is so important that we often feel that instead of being called the fourth it should be named the first dimension because cost must be considered first in all of our designing if our companies are to develop products that will excite the market.

    In manufacturing, we have to work with the two dimensions—material and energy—that the person studying pure science has to work with, but we have also to work with two additional dimensions. The third is very important, the customer; and the fourth, as we have said, is the cost factor. You may argue in any fashion you wish about the situation, but manufacturers must be sure that what they produce—and it may be the finest product that research can develop—is something that the buyer can afford to acquire. In other words, the people who produce products for sale in the open market must take into account the purchasing power of the customer in all aspects of the production of goods. Companies must be sure that what they develop they can afford to make and to sell at a reasonable profit. The fourth dimension is, therefore, critical.

    It has been said that the product produced by any industry is much more than the object itself. In a way, it is the packing case sent to the consumer in which are shipped the skilled labor of the maker and the thousand and one ideas that go into the product.

ENGLISH? NO ESCAPE!

69

PREVIEW WORDS

English subject taught study light minute forgotten escape graduated withdraw newspaper understand television matter slightly realize might benefit instruction understand process communicating errors department teacher assigned wrong yourself opportunities tool afterward doubt heart

WORDS

For a great many years, no doubt, you have looked upon English as a subject that is taught in school. You have not thought of it as a part of your life. While in school you are given English as a subject to study, and you think of it in that light. But do not for a minute think of it as just a school subject, something to be learned in school and then forgotten. Of all the subjects taught in school, English is the one from which you cannot escape all through your life.

You may think that, once you have graduated, you can just withdraw from this subject. But how can you? Can you leave school and not talk any more—not even read the newspaper, or read or write a letter, or understand the programs on your television set? Of course you cannot; and if you would only give the matter some real thought, or even if you would only think ever so slightly about it, you would realize that you might as well get all the benefit you can from the English instruction. You agree, of course, that you want people to understand what you say and what you write, and that you want to understand what others say and what they write. In a word, this process is called communicating.

If you think that your errors in English are sins against the English department at your school or the teacher assigned to help you, you are entirely wrong. Your errors in English are sins against yourself and your opportunities in life. Language is the tool with which you build your present and future life not only in school but afterward. There is no doubt about this matter; and in your heart, you must know that it is true.

(continued)

| 1 | 2 | 3 | 4 | 5 | 6 | 7 | 8 | 9 | 10 | 11 | 12 | 13 | 14 |

ENGLISH

69

RESEARCH: FRICTION, PAINTS

PREVIEW WORDS

friction research effect principally lubrication standard tables drawn theory lubricant number of pounds discovered quality basic idea about automobile industry durability method of application natural to assume main cause paint failure moisture wetting tiny cracks dew and the sun

Friction research has been less of a study of friction and a good deal more of a search for ways to reduce its effect principally through lubrication. Some years ago standard tables were drawn up on the theory that a good lubricant would stand a certain number of pounds per square inch. These tables were accepted for many years, but the research for ways to improve the effectiveness of lubricants continued. Before long, researchers had discovered methods for improving lubricating quality by more than six hundred per cent. This gain was made by changing the basic idea about the product. Because of this improvement, the cars of today are vastly better and will last much longer than the cars of past years. What will happen in the future, of course, cannot be predicted specifically, but we know that research on friction will continue.

Paints, which are also quite important to the automobile industry, have been the objects of research both as to durability of materials and as to methods of application. The auto industry has always had trouble with paints fading faster in the South than in the North. It has been only natural to assume that this fading was due to more intense rays of the sun, and much data was collected on the subject. But researchers have found that paint failure does not rise with the heat of the sun. In fact, the reverse is true. After much study, it was found that the main cause of early paint failure on autos was dew. Moisture wetting tiny cracks in paint from the bottom up causes both premature rusting and fading. Companies have since produced paints which resist cracking quite well.

TRY, TRY AGAIN

PREVIEW WORDS

```
piano perfect simply practice correctly concerts finest country ambition
remains thereby moral pasting prominent position suppose assume utterly
intention expert typist advise method completely experience guarantee
necessary outline divide progress athlete totally improvement quality
```

	WORDS	
The practice time I spent at the piano did not make perfect simply	14	660
because it was not perfect practice. If I had practiced correctly, I might	30	676
now be giving concerts in the finest music halls in the country.	43	689
However, I don't feel bad about it. In fact, I think I have lost all	57	703
ambition for that sort of thing; but the fact remains that the piano is	71	717
not my strong point and I know that it never will be.	82	728
Thereby hangs a moral which might be worth pasting in some	95	741
prominent position where you will not lose sight of it. I suppose it	109	755
is safe to assume that it is your intention to become an expert typist.	124	770
I would advise you to steer clear of my method of practicing piano	137	783
for, if you do not, you will land just where I did. In other words,	151	797
you will surely fail, utterly and completely. From my experience, I can	165	811
guarantee it.	168	814
I hardly believe it is necessary for me to outline the correct method	183	829
of practice for I think you know it as well as I do. At any rate, do	197	843
not divide your brain into two parts, one worrying because you do not	211	857
progress faster and the other wondering if your favorite athlete has set	226	872
a new record. Try to keep your mind totally on what you are doing	239	885
and do not think about anything else. If at the end of your practice	253	899
session at the typewriter you have not made some improvement, then	267	913
it is time that you set about to change your methods. Remember, it	280	926
is not the hours or days or weeks that you spend at the typewriter	294	940
that makes you a better typist. It is the quality of the time and the	308	954
use of the best methods that makes your practice and your progress	321	967
perfect.	323	969

| 1 | 2 | 3 | 4 | 5 | 6 | 7 | 8 | 9 | 10 | 11 | 12 | 13 | 14 |

PRACTICE (continued)

THE "CRANEBERRY"

PREVIEW WORDS

Thanksgiving American holiday Plymouth Colony American history settlers harvesting summer crops splendid foods enormous feast "craneberry" fruit red berries growing wild pink and white blossoms newcomers country plant northeast barrels popular difficult forked scoops damage delicate vines

	WORDS
You know very well that Thanksgiving is a truly American holiday.	14
It all started in the Plymouth colony on Cape Cod, which is known	27
to folks from Boston simply as The Cape. As you will recall from	40
your study of early American history, the settlers set aside a day	53
following their harvesting of all of the summer crops to give thanks	67
for the splendid foods that they had been able to grow. A feature of	81
the day was the enormous feast to which all of their Indian friends	94
were invited too.	98
An important part of the first Thanksgiving menu was a sauce	111
made from one of the most American of all fruits. It was called	124
"craneberry" then, but we have since changed the spelling to cranberry.	138
The Pilgrims had found the red berries growing wild and named the	151
fruit after its pink and white blossoms which resemble the head, bill,	165
and curved neck of a crane. So, naturally the newcomers to this	178
country who had never before seen such a plant called it the "cra-	191
neberry plant."	195
The plant grows well in the northeast, and it is recorded that ten	209
barrels of "craneberries" were sent to King Charles I as a gift from the	223
Plymouth colony. It took a long time, though, for the fruit to become	237
popular because it was so difficult for the settlers to harvest.	250
Flowers appear on the cranberry vines in May or June, and the	263
berries ripen during August and September and vary in color from light	277
pink to dark purple. Forked scoops are still used to harvest the berries	292
for no other method has yet been found that does not damage the	305
delicate vines. The berries must be gathered when ripe and dry.	318

| 1 | 2 | 3 | 4 | 5 | 6 | 7 | 8 | 9 | 10 | 11 | 12 | 13 | 14 |

YOU DON'T SUCCEED... 67

PREVIEW WORDS

trying piano practiced result choice hymn hung escape untimely barely trouble gamut scales learned sixteen sample foreign meant understand directions language expression butter parsnips supporting family crank sensible conclusion probably grinding monkey keyboard reason failure

WORDS

When I was trying to learn to play the piano, I practiced. You can bet that I practiced every day and every week and every month. There was some result. Even now if I were given the choice of having to play a hymn or being hung, I think I could escape an untimely end. 15 335 / 29 349 / 42 362 / 56 376

What was the trouble? I ran the gamut of scales and learned many things. Today when I see a note with a black face and two tails, I know that it takes sixteen of him to make a good sample. I learned not only my notes and how to play them, but I also learned what all the foreign words meant. I never could understand why all the directions were given in a foreign language. Anyway, I learned what those words stood for and I knew when to play loud and when to play soft; when to slow down and when to speed up. I even tried to play the notes with expression. 70 390 / 83 403 / 97 417 / 111 431 / 124 444 / 138 458 / 152 472 / 165 485 / 170 490

All such things are nice to know, of course, but they do not butter the parsnips, as the poet says. After supporting that music professor for a few years, the family came to the sensible conclusion that if I ever made a name for myself in the world of music, it would probably be grinding the crank of a hand organ with a monkey by my side. 184 504 / 199 519 / 213 533 / 226 546 / 239 559

I was a failure and the reason is not hard to find. I practiced, all right, always one hour a day. The trouble was I always had one eye on the keyboard and one on the clock. With one half of my mind, I tried to remember that a note with a dot is worth half as much again as a note without a dot; and the other half of my mind wondered where my friends were going fishing at four o'clock and if they knew where to get worms. 254 574 / 268 588 / 281 601 / 295 615 / 308 628 / 322 642 / 326 646

(continued)

| 1 | 2 | 3 | 4 | 5 | 6 | 7 | 8 | 9 | 10 | 11 | 12 | 13 | 14 |

PRACTICE *(continued)*

AN OUTDOOR HAZARD

25

PREVIEW WORDS

scientists doctors toxic substances adjective derived toxicus toxicum poison principally coating arrows uncommon poison oak poison ivy oil excreted shrubs chemical irritant soot smoke animals reaction confined potential victims special extracts susceptibility individual immunize

WORDS

Scientists and doctors who are concerned by such things have learned a great deal in recent years about the many plants which contain toxic substances. The word toxic is an adjective and is derived from the Latin words toxicus and toxicum. In those days, these words meant poison, the kind which was principally used for coating the tips of arrows used in warfare and which made getting struck by an arrow even more deadly. Today, the word toxic means just about the same thing except that the practice of coating arrows with poison is uncommon.

Plants which contain toxic substances, however, are quite common; and they can cause an enormous amount of trouble for the unfortunate ones who come in contact with them. Of all the toxic plants, poison oak and poison ivy are the most common. An oil excreted by these shrubs contains a chemical which is the noxious agent that affects so many.

The irritant is not spread by the wind, as is often supposed; but it can be carried in soot, smoke, or burning plants as well as on tools, clothes, or the fur of animals. The reaction is usually confined to the skin, and over half of all adults are potential victims, although the rate is much higher for children. Skin tests are now available which use special extracts taken from the poisonous plants, and the amount of susceptibility of any individual can be measured with accuracy.

Medical preparations are available which help to immunize, but the very best means of avoiding the misery of poison ivy is to learn to recognize the shiny three-leaf plants and stay far away from them.

| 1 | 2 | 3 | 4 | 5 | 6 | 7 | 8 | 9 | 10 | 11 | 12 | 13 | 14 |

IF AT FIRST . . .

66

PREVIEW WORDS

essentials expert business practice desired reached somebody perfect
believed fifteen different ratio fourteen listed proper experience
instance mother pianist handed professor doctors prescription medicine
exercise favorite detective baseball difference lesson pointed clock

	WORDS
One of the essentials which go into the making of an expert in	14
our business is practice, much practice, and then some more practice.	28
The desired end cannot be reached without it. When I was a lad, we	41
used to write in a copy book. The copy was placed at the top of the	55
page by somebody who was expert at that sort of thing, and one of	68
those lines was "practice makes perfect." I believed it then, and I	82
believe it now.	86
The trouble is that there are too many kinds of practice. There are	100
at least fifteen different kinds of practice, running from good to bad	115
in about the ratio of one good and fourteen bad. I have listed them	128
all in proper order and speak from experience.	138
I have done a lot of practicing in my time. For instance, when I	152
was about ten years old, my mother got the idea that I was going to	166
become a pianist—not just a pianist but a very good one. She handed	180
me over to a professor who was going to teach me how to play the	193
piano. Like all doctors, he gave me a prescription, and the bottle bore	207
the label "exercise." I took the medicine for an hour a day by the	221
clock. Never did I get so much real exercise out of anything else in	235
my life.	237
I was a good boy and did what my mother told me to do, although	251
I must admit I did not enjoy it. However, every day when the hands	264
of the clock pointed to three, my mother would call me to come inside	278
and take my lesson. It made no difference whether I was playing my	292
best game of baseball or reading my favorite detective story, I knew	306
when the call came that I would answer it and then do my very best.	320

(continued)

| 1 | 2 | 3 | 4 | 5 | 6 | 7 | 8 | 9 | 10 | 11 | 12 | 13 | 14 |

PRACTICE

BELLS 26

PREVIEW WORDS

Paul Revere church historic midnight achieved New England early middle century trickly molders riggers equipment cooling tempered particularly violently Liberty Bell vigorous ringing inexperienced bell ringers metal mixture copper proportion fusing delicate processed suspension resonant

WORDS

    Although Paul Revere is less known for his church bells than for his historic midnight ride, the Revere bells achieved fame in many parts of New England during the early and middle years of the last century. — 14, 28, 41, 44

    The casting and hanging of bells was a tricky business then, and both are still considered difficult by molders and riggers, even with the most modern equipment available today. In the days of Revere, bells were usually cast in the open air, and the slow cooling which tempered them was particularly difficult. Many of the bells were rung too violently at the start which caused them to crack. This was the fate of the most famous Liberty Bell which is supposed to have been cracked from some too vigorous ringing by inexperienced bell ringers. — 58, 72, 86, 100, 113, 127, 139, 153

    You may not know it, but bell metal is a proper mixture of copper and tin in the proportion of about four parts of copper to one part of tin. The fusing of these metals and the tempering of the bell after casting were and are delicate processes which determine the quality of the bell. Most Revere bells weighed less than a ton, and they were usually hung on wooden yokes with a wheel. Those who know maintain vigorously that the wooden type suspension, although less rigid than the metal yoke, gives the bell a purer and more resonant tone than the metal type. — 167, 180, 194, 209, 222, 235, 249, 263, 266

    Bells are no longer an important part of community life, but in Paul Revere's day, his bells in New England communities called generations to worship, rang at sunrise to awaken people, at noon to tell them to go home to lunch, and at sunset to conclude work. — 279, 292, 306, 319

| 1 | 2 | 3 | 4 | 5 | 6 | 7 | 8 | 9 | 10 | 11 | 12 | 13 | 14 |

BELLS

A WHALE OF A YARN

PREVIEW WORDS

passed friend pulled wondered remembered revolver pocket knocked oar
afraid foolish spoil perfectly moment surely punched fist believe stem
stern finally blessed caution eighty respect Jonah family neighbors
referred yarn fault happen beside seemed ought supper doctor really

	WORDS	

As the whale passed by, my friend pulled in the oar on that side of the boat, and we wondered what would happen next. Then I remembered that I had a revolver in my pocket, and I pulled it out and was going to try a shot for luck. However, my friend knocked the gun out of my hand with an oar, saying that we might want to go fishing again. He was afraid the whale beside us might flip his tail, and it was foolish to spoil a perfectly good boat. So I put my gun away for the moment.

It seemed to me as if it surely would touch the side of our boat. I put out my hand and tried to push it away, but I did not have much luck. Then I got mad and punched it with my fist as hard as I could. Come to think of it, I believe I ought to have a medal for being the only man who ever punched a live whale in the ribs and lived to tell about it. Now that I am older I know how lucky I am, too.

Finally came the tail, and after seeing it, I blessed the caution of my friend. I will take my solemn oath that the whale was well over eighty feet from stem to stern. Since that day, you can believe that I have had much respect for Jonah. So help me, if his whale was as big as the one I punched, he could have taken his whole family with him and still had space to rent to his very close friends and neighbors.

That is the story, the true story, mind you, as I told it that night at the supper table. That is the story that the doctor referred to as "a whale of a yarn." Maybe what he really meant to say was that it was "the yarn of a whale." If so, I have no fault to find with him.

| 1 | 2 | 3 | 4 | 5 | 6 | 7 | 8 | 9 | 10 | 11 | 12 | 13 | 14 |

THE WHALE *(continued)*

DUFFY'S SPUR

PREVIEW WORDS

something inside creates hustle ripe define churns refer practically spur of ambition outcome behind sharp animal question both ends meet chase the tip two-foot ring hours on end bit of difference Duffy heaven high degree puzzled curious figure out marvelous miracle satisfy admit

There is something inside of most humans which creates a desire for big things and which makes them get up and hustle to do things when the time is ripe for the doing of them. If you were asked to define this something which churns within, you might refer to it very practically as the spur of ambition. It is hard to believe that much was ever done in the world, whether the outcome was big or little, that did not have behind it the spur of ambition. We may not be aware of the fact at the time, but if we will hunt long enough, we will be sure to find that spur sticking us every time we set our minds on doing anything. Very often the spur is so sharp that it keeps us going whether we want to or not.

Humans are not the only animals that feel the spur of ambition—there is no question about that. I once had a dog who was so ambitious to make both ends meet that he would chase the tip of his tail around a two-foot ring for hours on end. He never caught it, so far as I know, but that did not make a bit of difference to Duffy. He kept at it up to the day of his death. The ambition never left Duffy, and if there is a heaven for dogs of high degree, I am sure he is there and is still on the job.

I was always a little puzzled over that curious ambition, for I could not figure out where the spur came from. Nor could I understand what good it would do Duffy if he did on some marvelous day catch the end of his tail. I used to hope that he would by some miracle do it some day so that I might satisfy my curiosity, but he never did, at least to my knowledge.

| 1 | 2 | 3 | 4 | 5 | 6 | 7 | 8 | 9 | 10 | 11 | 12 | 13 | 14 |

A BOAT AND A WHALE

PREVIEW WORDS

meant anything personal compliment quotation remarks sermon happened
memory details yesterday misty bluefish several dense hulls vessels
masts phantom secret mission blowing whale although behind straight
veered skipped biting fling headed anyway friend extend missed foot

WORDS

Now, what do you think of that? Of course, he may not have meant anything personal and may have wanted to compliment me on my story. Maybe the quotation from David had nothing to do with his remarks. Anyway, I was the one who asked about the sermon. As for the story, it was a true tale or I would not have told it. While it is a story that happened a good many years ago, I pride myself on a good memory for details. I can see it all just as though it were yesterday.	13 26 40 53 68 81 94 96	336 349 363 376 391 404 417 419
One misty morning toward the end of July, a friend and I set out in our boat to do some fishing. The bluefish had really been biting well for several days, and I wanted one or two for dinner. There was a very dense fog resting on the sea. However, it did not extend high enough above the water to hide anything but the hulls of the vessels; and as they went by their masts stuck up above the fog as though they were part of phantom ships on their way out to sea for their own secret mission.	110 124 138 152 166 179 192 196	433 447 461 475 489 502 515 519
We had not gone very far from the shore when I heard a sound that I knew well. It was the blowing of a whale, and he seemed to be only a few feet away although I could not see him because of the fog. Just as I was about to fling my bait out again, I saw a thing that I had never seen before. Its head was at least ten feet long, and behind the head was a body so long that it was lost in the fog before I could see the end. It was headed straight on course for our boat. Then, just when it seemed we would be hit, that whale veered to the right and missed us by about a foot. You can bet my heart skipped a few beats.	210 223 237 251 266 280 295 308 322	533 546 560 574 589 603 618 631 645

(continued)

| 1 | 2 | 3 | 4 | 5 | 6 | 7 | 8 | 9 | 10 | 11 | 12 | 13 | 14 |

THE WHALE *(continued)*

GRABBING THE COATTAILS

PREVIEW WORDS

ambitions bigger and better times mess of things Napoleon throne France high in the heavens blaze history written stone coffin St. Helena empire crumbled indelibly Arnold bravest garret outcast exceptions risen fallen ripest furthest colors bundles coattails beast choice grabbing apt loss

WORDS

There have been people with ambitions so big that they have lifted	14
this old world of ours out of a rut and set it rolling on its way to	28
bigger and better times. But there have been times when the individuals	42
who had such ambitions made more or less a mess of things.	54
It was such an ambition that put Napoleon on the throne of France	68
and set his star so high in the heavens that it will blaze there so long	82
as history shall be written. But his ambition also made Napoleon fit	96
a nice stone coffin at St. Helena, and both he and his empire long ago	110
crumbled into dust. It was such an ambition that wrote indelibly the	124
name of Arnold high in the list of early American heroes as one of	137
the bravest where all were brave. But it also made him die in a garret,	152
an outcast among outcasts, the meanest thing where all was mean.	164
These two fellows were not exceptions. There have been those	177
without number who have both risen and fallen under the spur of	190
ambition. The ripest fruit is to be found at the top of the tree. But	204
as that top is furthest from the ground, so those reaching it have the	218
furthest to fall if they let go, and get most badly hurt if they do	231
indeed fall.	234
There are more kinds of ambition than there are cats, and each	247
kind comes in a good many colors and tied up in all sorts of bundles.	261
If you feel that you must try to grab the coattails of an ambition, it	275
is wise to get a look at the face of the beast before it grabs you.	289
Although ambitions are lying about all the time and you can always	303
make a choice, grabbing the wrong kind is apt to cause the loss of	316
both time and money.	321

| 1 | 2 | 3 | 4 | 5 | 6 | 7 | 8 | 9 | 10 | 11 | 12 | 13 | 14 |

THE BEGINNING OF A YARN

63

PREVIEW WORDS

Sunday guests country unusually quiet gazed ceiling puffing briar own thoughts silence worried anything spoil insult watching quite sermon quaint village without started hinting remarked text David liars yarn paused whale moment mouth behind meant private nothing doctor supper

	WORDS
As we sat there that Sunday morning, the only guests in the little	14
country hotel, it seemed to me that the doctor was unusually quiet.	28
For a long time he had sat there and gazed at the ceiling, puffing	42
away at his briar pipe. He had a far away look in his eyes, but he	55
really saw nothing; the man was busy with private thoughts.	67
His silence worried me, for we were going on a fishing trip the	81
next morning and I did not want anything to spoil our plans. I felt	95
that it would be more or less of an insult to ask the doctor if he did	109
not feel well, but after watching him for quite a while, I thought I	123
would make him talk a little and thus drive away what I took to be	136
a fit of good old blues. To that end, I asked him what he thought of	150
the sermon both of us had heard that morning in the quaint little	164
village church.	167
For a long time, he just sat and looked at me without saying a	181
word. Then he got up and started toward the door, hinting that it was	195
getting late and that we had to start early in the morning. When he	209
got to the door, he turned and remarked, "As for that sermon, it was	222
very good; but the best part of it lay in the text. You remember that	237
he read about the man by the name of David who said that all men	250
are liars." He paused a minute and then added as he went out, "Say,	263
that was a whale of a yarn you told at the supper table last night."	277
Then he shut the door behind him, and I heard his steps as he went	291
up the stairs to bed. For a moment or two, I sat there with my mouth	305
open ready to ask just what he meant, but I knew I would just have	318
to wait for morning.	323

(continued)

|1 |2 |3 |4 |5 |6 |7 |8 |9 |10 |11 |12 |13 |14 |

THE WHALE

THE POOR CHAMELEON

PREVIEW WORDS

extent radical occupation position debate determined to exploit wings making the jumps disappointment disaster chameleon sort lizard possesses whatever surroundings straightway Montana goldenrod autumn effort bright struck Scotch plaid reputation assume acute heart disease suggest alter

To what extent you folks starting out on a business career can make radical changes either in occupation or position is a question for some debate. If you are determined to exploit your wings, you should always count the cost of changes and pick out good landing places before making the jumps. Too many and too varied changes are very likely to end in disappointment at the least and possibly disaster at the worst.

Maybe you have heard the story of the lad and the chameleon. As you know, the chameleon, a sort of lizard, possesses the admirable trait of being able to change its color quickly so that it is always in accord with whatever may be its surroundings. It is said that the boy had one of these lizards and used to experiment to test its ability to change and survive satisfactorily the changes. He put it upon a bit of blue cloth and straightway that chameleon was bluer than the big skies of Montana. Then he tried it on a piece of yellow stuff, and it at once turned the color of the goldenrod in autumn with no effort at all.

The lad was delighted and a bright idea having struck him, he brought out a piece of Scotch plaid that had seven or eight different tints. That lizard tried to live up to its reputation for change and made an effort to assume all those colors at once. The changes were too much for the poor chameleon, and acute heart failure, or something just as bad, set in; and the poor thing died right then and there. All of which suggests that to jump from one thing to another with no reason other than to alter relationships with your surroundings could be a mistake.

| 1 | 2 | 3 | 4 | 5 | 6 | 7 | 8 | 9 | 10 | 11 | 12 | 13 | 14 |

LEAVE THAT CACTUS ALONE!

PREVIEW WORDS

cactus plaything iron poet remarked thorn botany concerned simile thousand moderate estimate sometimes trunks pancake referred bayonet clusters generally uncomfortable happens stumble bunch brilliant blossom August September ceased beauty pricking porcupine system

The cactus has not been a good plaything since the day when men wore iron clothes. The poet who remarked that every rose had its thorn was a back number so far as his botany was concerned; for if he had only used the cactus as a simile, he could have added a thousand thorns and still have been very moderate in his estimate.

Sometimes the cactus grows out of the trunks of trees and sometimes you will find them on the edge of the big pancake leaf I have referred to before. Sometimes they form the small end of a bayonet a foot or more long. These grow in clusters, and they are generally more or less uncomfortable if one happens to stumble and sit down on a bunch of them. And that reminds me of a story which you just might enjoy.

Once when I was driving through the desert, I saw a cactus that had a brilliant red blossom. It was so pretty that I stopped the car to pick it. I did not have any trouble picking it. I will never forget that it was early in May when I got hold of that flower and the middle of August before I ceased to rave over its beauty. But it was late in September before I finally removed the last one of those pricking things from my system. You see, when I bent over to pick the flower, there were other cactus plants that I did not notice. Then when I got up, the seat of my trousers looked like the back of a young porcupine. You can be sure I picked out those that were in sight, but there were so many hidden in the fabric that I only discovered them when they dug their way into me. I finally had to burn the pants to get rid of them.

| 1 | 2 | 3 | 4 | 5 | 6 | 7 | 8 | 9 | 10 | 11 | 12 | 13 | 14 |

CACTUS *(continued)*

THIS FABLE TEACHES...

PREVIEW WORDS

strenuous suspicion valuable Latin conversation anywhere ancient volume Aesop themselves express puncture consciousness wandering humiliation brighten qualities personality yarns unique particular heroine turtle jackrabbit amazing difficulties expected footsteps ordinary common

As I turn and look back over a long and strenuous career, I cannot avoid a mean suspicion that I wasted a good deal of valuable time in trying to master the study of Latin, because I have never found it useful in conversation, and not much anywhere else. But there is one thing I remember about that ancient language that was not at all unpleasant, and that was a little volume of stories by Aesop.

His stories were short and to the point. Not only were they interesting in themselves but they seem also to have been written for the express purpose of pointing a moral which was attached to the end. The moral was intended to puncture my inner consciousness, lead my wandering steps out of the valley of humiliation and brighten up certain qualities which it was thought might be lacking in my personality. I never really believed those yarns, and to this day I doubt whether they were true.

They were unique, though, in one particular, which was that in every instance the hero or heroine was a mud turtle, a jackrabbit, a donkey, or some other animal. They were always getting into the most amazing difficulties so much so that I could never get it through my head why I should be expected to follow in their footsteps. To a boy possessed of ordinary common sense, they looked foolish. But I read them because they were a part of my daily grind; and as I have said, I rather liked them even if they did end up with a sentence which, translated, meant "this fable teaches." In some ways, I wish I could have met Mr. Aesop; for he was a good storyteller, which is just what I would like to be.

THE BLOOMING CACTUS

PREVIEW WORDS

interesting cactus alike variations differ extent doubt almost desert
searched different wandered thumb towering trunk extends managed tints
country separate crowned prettiest flowers yellow rival rainbow apex
beauty varieties clusters pancake favorite flowering growing suppose

    One interesting thing about the cactus is that there are no two that are alike. It is not so with the oak, the elm, and the maple, which are only variations of one single plan and do not differ from one another to any great extent. But cactus trees are all different, and I doubt whether you could find a pair of twin trees, two that were almost alike, if you searched a whole lifetime.

    I do not know how many kinds of cactus trees there are, but I have never wandered about in the desert without coming across one I had never seen before. You can get any size you want from that of your thumb to a towering trunk that extends thirty or maybe fifty feet into the air.

    I have always managed to visit the cactus country in the spring, and at that time, each separate bush or tree is crowned with the prettiest flowers to be found anywhere. They are red, yellow, and blue and with all the tints between. Their colors really rival the rainbow. It is odd to see a tall tree with a trunk twenty inches through at the base and more than half that at the top, with only a single scarlet blossom at the apex. While it is true that many times a cactus tree has only one blossom, it is a blossom that rivals all others in beauty and surpasses some.

    Of the smaller varieties of cacti, the flowers are often found in clusters, sometimes growing out of a large stem and then again out of the edge of a leaf. At any rate, I suppose you would call them leaves, but to me they look for all the world like a great pancake. As you can see, the cactus is one of my favorite flowering trees.

(continued)

| 1 | 2 | 3 | 4 | 5 | 6 | 7 | 8 | 9 | 10 | 11 | 12 | 13 | 14 |

CACTUS *(continued)*

SEASICK AND THE SEA 31

PREVIEW WORDS

memory remember experiences matter seasick doctor serious trouble
related middle plumb interior white overtime stomach calm invited
sixty thirty rough everyone misery thinking getting however accept
finally reason truth somewhere worst friends glass became without

	WORDS
I do not know how old I was when I first began to have a deep	13
love of the sea and all that is in it. While I have a good memory,	27
it does not go back so far as to remember that. I have read every sea	41
tale that I could lay my hands on and have even tried to write some	55
myself from my own experiences. I wish I could tell you that the sea	69
loves me back, but the truth of the matter is that I am very often	82
seasick.	84
My doctor tells me that being seasick is not very serious. Then he	99
says my trouble is related to my middle ear, a thing that he says I	112
keep somewhere in my head to let me know when I am out of plumb.	125
I do not know much about my interior as a rule, but when it comes	139
to my middle ear, I do know that it works overtime when it gets a	152
chance to show just what it can do. The worst part of it is that I	165
never know when I am going to be hit by it. The sea may be calm	178
when we leave port, but my stomach is anything but calm in a short	192
while.	193
Once some friends of mine hired a tug to go out after codfish.	207
They invited me to go along, and we went out about sixty miles from	221
port. The first thirty miles out, the sea was like glass and I loved it;	236
but the next thirty miles were pretty rough, and my middle ear and	250
I became very upset. I was glad everyone left me to my own misery.	263
We made the trip a good many times, and I kept thinking each	276
time I would be able to make it without getting seasick. However, such	291
was not the case; I finally came to accept the idea that what is to be	305
will be, so there was no reason I should be upset about being seasick.	318

(continued)

| 1 | 2 | 3 | 4 | 5 | 6 | 7 | 8 | 9 | 10 | 11 | 12 | 13 | 14 |

THE SEA

CACTUS COUNTRY

PREVIEW WORDS

believe forget feeling cactus sight memory happened yesterday quite plainly driving motel decided straight through crossing desert vast vegetation sagebrush mesquite appeared something expanse reminded gallows beheld scene another fascination disease attacked hundreds

I do not believe that I will ever forget the feeling that came over me the very first time I ever saw a cactus. It was a good many years ago, but the sight of my first cactus is just as fresh in my memory as if it had happened only yesterday. I can still see it quite plainly.

My friend and I were driving across the country and, in order to save money on motel bills, we decided to drive straight through. It was his turn to drive and my turn to sleep, which was fine with me since we were driving at night. When I opened my eyes early in the morning, I saw we were crossing the desert. There was the flat, dry, brown dirt just as far as the eye could see. There was no vegetation except sagebrush and mesquite, none of which grew much higher than the head of a man. There appeared to be little food for the soul or body of man.

Then I saw something that stood alone in the vast expanse—something that reminded me of a gallows tree—but I had seen pictures of it in books and knew that for the first time my eyes beheld a cactus. Then came another and another, and they came on the scene by the hundreds all day long. I could not take my eyes off them, and my only regret was that we could not stop to examine them.

There was a fascination about them that I cannot explain. I know it was there then and I know that it has never left me to this day. Year after year since that time, I have made the same journey and always with the same desire to see those cactus trees. It is not a disease that has attacked me alone, for my friends tell me they love them too.

(continued)

SEA CREATURES

32

PREVIEW WORDS

learned secrets neighbor whale slowly stretch lazy length surface watched kitten jumping bulk deadly enemy swordfish happiest obliged hungry bother shark quarter lamprey eel appeared neither fowl oyster herring mussel lobster assortment jaws huge strain dinner quite clock

I have said that I love the sea; and I not only love it, but I have learned many of its secrets. I have been near neighbor to the whale as he came slowly up from the deep to stretch his lazy length, at least forty and more feet of it, on the surface, and blow off steam like a train. I have watched him at play like a kitten and have seen him when he was not at play but was jumping twenty feet into the air in an effort to land his huge bulk on his deadly enemy the swordfish.

Taken all in all, to my mind the whale has the happiest life of any animal there is. He is not tied down to one spot or obliged to keep his eye on the clock; but the road is wide open to him to go where he pleases to the ends of the earth. If he gets hungry, all he has to do is to open his huge jaws and strain his big dinner out of all the small things that live in the sea. The price of sugar does not bother him.

And I know the fishes, most of them, from the big shark down to the tiny things not a quarter of an inch long. I like most of them, but there are a few with which I am not quite so well pleased. The other day I was fishing from the rocks when I got hold of a lamprey eel. He was a big fellow whose head appeared to be almost as large as a football.

Then there are those things in the sea that are neither fish, flesh, fowl, nor red herring. These are the things that live in shells, such as the oyster, the clam, the crab, and the mussel. And the greatest of all this assortment is the lobster with his robe of blazing fire whose claim to fame is well known in all the fine restaurants of the world.

| 1 | 2 | 3 | 4 | 5 | 6 | 7 | 8 | 9 | 10 | 11 | 12 | 13 | 14 |

THE SEA (continued)

LOST OR MISLAID? 59

PREVIEW WORDS

really truly except everybody stroll discovered trouble buildings matter stopped finally missed remember blocks imagine grateful silence started mislaid difference between Boston overnight decided breakfast efforts frustrating happened foolish guessed directions despair scared

Now, as I started to say at the outset, I have been lost; and I am going to tell you all about it. Keep in mind that I was really and truly lost and not simply mislaid, for there is a vast deal of difference between the two. When a thing is lost, no one knows where it is; but when a thing is mislaid, everybody may know where it is except the one who mislaid it. I know, because I lost my hotel in Boston when I was visiting there once.

Well, of course, it was not really my hotel, so you might say that I mislaid it. After staying overnight at that hotel I decided it would be nice to take a short stroll before breakfast. When I tried to find my way back, it was then that I discovered that I must have mislaid it. What made my efforts to get back even more frustrating was that I had no trouble seeing the tall hotel above all the other buildings. But no matter how many different turns I made, I just could not find my way back home. I wonder if this has ever happened to you. After a while, you begin to feel a little foolish and at the same time a little scared.

Finally, after trying for almost an hour to find my lost hotel on my own, I stopped a nice woman and asked for her help. She told me how to get there and added that I could not miss it. You guessed it; I missed it. Then there were the directions from a nice man, but I still could not find my lost hotel. In despair and almost in tears by now, I took a cab. I still remember the look on the driver's face as we drove the four blocks to my hotel. He took my money without saying a word, and I was very grateful for his silence.

| 1 | 2 | 3 | 4 | 5 | 6 | 7 | 8 | 9 | 10 | 11 | 12 | 13 | 14 |

LOST *(continued)*

FISHING ON THE FARM

PREVIEW WORDS

forward vacation summer friend memories arrived parents straight morning swiftly together corners fishing clothes hurried breakfast winked understood harness driving garden during excuse school farm across looking nodded eating worms minutes expert whether outdoors

	WORDS
All of us look forward to summer vacation when school is out	13
and we can do all kinds of fun things. Let me tell you about a	26
summer I spent with my friends on a farm, for the memories are still	39
very dear to me.	43
The trip from the city took a long time. By the time my parents	56
and I arrived at the farm, the hour was so late that I went straight	70
to bed. When I woke up the next morning, I looked out the window	83
and saw that the clouds were moving swiftly across the sky. They	97
were dirty-looking clouds and were getting together in corners in a	110
way which led me to think that there would be rain before the day	123
was done.	126
Now, on a farm when it is too wet to work out of doors, there	139
is but one thing to do and that is to go fishing. So I got into my	153
clothes just as fast as I could and hurried down to the breakfast table.	167
As we were eating, I winked my left eye at my friend across the	180
table. He understood it and nodded his head and got up and went out	194
to the barn to harness the horses. That was what made it so much	207
fun to go fishing when you live on a farm, for no one would think	220
of driving the family car down to the creek to go fishing.	233
I packed a lunch for my friend and me, and then we went out	246
into the garden to dig the worms. All of the above took but a few	259
minutes for each of us was an expert in his own way. This was not	272
the first time we had been fishing together. In fact, we went fishing	287
about every day we could during vacation, whether it was too wet to	300
work outdoors or not. You can bet we used every excuse in the book.	314

(continued)

| 1 | 2 | 3 | 4 | 5 | 6 | 7 | 8 | 9 | 10 | 11 | 12 | 13 | 14 |

LOST AND FOUND   58

PREVIEW WORDS

their pleasure lately enjoy programs interesting certainly known sometimes always finders enjoy papers heart relates column piece lost and found offered lucky tempted prevents wasting better happy odds nicest together imagine section provides something rightful

WORDS

  There are times when it seems only a short time ago that I used to like to read the lost and found column in the daily papers. I took a great deal of pleasure in trying to piece out the story of each lost thing, for I was sure the story was there if I could only get a hold of it. You will note that I say I used to like to read about those things. Lately, I find that I do not like to read that column any more for all the fun has gone out of it. Now, about the only time I turn to it is when there is nothing better to do or there are no good programs on TV. Maybe one day I will once again enjoy making up nice stories about all of those interesting things that have been lost and found.

  At any rate, reading the lost and found column certainly is not dull. It is made up of all the odds and ends of every known thing on the face of the earth. Sometimes the rewards which are offered to the lucky finders are so big I am tempted to stop what I am doing and do a little hunting on my own. One of the things that prevents me from doing this is that there are always more things lost than there are that are found, and I know in my heart that I would just be wasting my time.

  Yet, one of the nicest things about the lost and found column is that it provides just the right kind of section to get people together who have lost or found something. I can just imagine how many happy people there are each day when that which was lost or found is once again returned to its rightful owner. When you think of all the bad news in the papers these days, you might say this is a happy column.

(continued)

| 1 | 2 | 3 | 4 | 5 | 6 | 7 | 8 | 9 | 10 | 11 | 12 | 13 | 14 |

LOST *(continued)*   58

FISHING AND LUCK 34

PREVIEW WORDS

stuff together horse friend almanac sign fishing anything journey creek
before concerned something wrong forgot knife started luck horses back
good-bye however between looked unhappy indeed neighbor across trouble
omens asked certain goat someone camping avoid breath happened catch

I put all of our stuff together and was about to get on the horse when my friend said he would go and hunt up the almanac and see if the sign was right to go fishing. When he came back and did not say anything, I was sure that it was all right so we kept on our journey to the creek.

Before we had gone a mile, I began to think that so far as signs were concerned, there was something wrong. In the first place, I forgot my knife and we had to go back to get it. I did not like to do that for to turn back after one has started on a journey is bad luck. At least, I have been told that it is bad luck. And then Dick, the old house dog, had an idea that something was wrong. As a rule when we went away, he would run out before the horses and go with us to the gate. Then he would bid us goodbye. However, this time he stood in the door with his tail between his legs and looked very sad.

When we got to the house of a neighbor, a black cat ran across the road in front of us; and you all know what that means. By this time, I felt sure that if signs and omens stood for anything, I was in for a lot of trouble. You can bet I was certain of it when I asked my friend to tell me where he found the sign in the almanac and he said "the goat." I knew someone would get mine before the day was over, but it was no use to turn back. I knew that if bad luck was camping on my trail this day, there was no way I could avoid it. It could catch me just as well at the house as it could out in the woods or on the bank of the creek. So I just made up my mind to hold my breath and see what happened.

| 1 | 2 | 3 | 4 | 5 | 6 | 7 | 8 | 9 | 10 | 11 | 12 | 13 | 14 |

FISHING (continued)

LOST

PREVIEW WORDS

chair thought stolen right short hearing ought temper lifetime prize four-letter trouble length likely remind child typical change agree gloomy better attention biggest school restroom refreshing missing sheep agree matter little confesses alley admit itself dictionary

	WORDS
Of course, it is now all over and done with; and in such a case,	14
one ought to let it go and forget it. Yet, it is hard to do that, no	28
matter how I try. Every time I sit down in my nice easy chair at	41
home, it all comes back to me and makes me sad and gloomy all over	54
again. The thought has come to me that if I tell you about it, I will	68
feel much better—just as a small child does who has stolen some	81
change and comes back and confesses the deed and seeks forgiveness	95
from his elders.	99
But before I begin, I want to call your attention to one of the	112
biggest four-letter words in the dictionary. Now, I admit it is not the	127
typical four-letter word you are used to hearing at school or in the	141
alley or one that you are likely to see on the restroom walls. It is not	156
a word that is likely to get you in trouble, no matter who hears you	169
use it. The fact in itself ought to be rather refreshing these days. It	184
is a short word that packs more real trouble than many of the others	198
of the same length. The word is "lost."	207
Now, the dictionary says that when a thing is lost, it is missing.	221
It goes on to tell about a lost sheep and a lost limb and a lost soul.	236
We all know how a prize can be lost—or even a temper, for that	248
matter. In fact, with very little effort, all of us could make up a long	263
list of things that we have lost in our lifetime.	274
The point is that none of us needs a dictionary to remind us of	287
the things we have lost. After you have read what I am going to say,	301
see if you will agree with me that it is not a nice thing for anyone	315
to be lost.	318

(continued)

| 1 | 2 | 3 | 4 | 5 | 6 | 7 | 8 | 9 | 10 | 11 | 12 | 13 | 14 |

THE WINNER 35

PREVIEW WORDS

poet lover ought willing myself whether certain winner fellow defeat contest often sometimes receives medals picture point things reasons being thought uncover definition prize persistent effort struggle attain obtain desired prevail supposed succeed language gained trial

Some poet once wrote that all the world loves a lover, and being a poet—the kind of person who ought to know about such things—most of us are willing to go along with the idea. I do not know myself whether it is true or not, but of one thing I am certain: all the world loves a winner, even the one who goes down to defeat in the contest.

Winners get a lot of fame and often some money. Sometimes they receive medals and everyone knows their name. Their picture is in the paper, and people point to them on the street. It is for all of these things that we love a winner, and for the same reasons we would also like to win. Such being the case, it seems to me that we might just give a little thought to the matter and try to uncover something that will teach us just what it is to be a winner, so that we can win too.

I have a large book on my desk which is supposed to have in it all the words in our language. When I am in doubt about a word, I go to that book and look it up. I did that just now and found that to win anything means that one must succeed in an effort or must prevail in a contest. One must attain a desired end or obtain a thing by long and very persistent effort and struggle. The definition also stated that the thing which is gained, the thing which is handed to you as the reward for your effort or struggle, is called a prize. In fact, it certainly would seem that there is nothing done in this old world of ours today, no work or effort of any kind, no trial, no struggle, that does not have as the goal in mind a reward or prize that makes the effort worthwhile.

(continued)

SENIOR OWLS 56

PREVIEW WORDS

terribly senior generation common sense daily routines firmly settled dangerous established well-behaved abroad venture youngster has-been greater mistake hue strange and bewildering glare blinding flutter about hither and thither stumbling shotgun minus pretty feathers extracting

   It is not terribly difficult to be a senior owl—that is, an older one among many of a younger generation—but it does call for a certain degree of common sense. Most senior owls, but possibly not all, have spent their lives in daily routines that have become, over the years, firmly settled habits. It is always a dangerous thing to try to break established routines, and the senior owls should have learned the fact.

   Well-behaved owls, as you know, wander abroad only by night, and few venture forth by day. Sometimes, however, a senior owl will go into the bright light of the sun perhaps to prove to the youngster owls that he is no has-been and that he is up to the minute in his thinking and in his skills. There is no greater mistake that an owl can make, and all of the older owls should know better. The very trees in the great forest in which the owl has lived take on a hue different from that they have presented to him before, and this is strange and bewildering. The glare of the sun will be blinding, and the poor owl will very likely flutter about aimlessly, hither and thither. And although it doesn't always happen, there is a good chance of stumbling into the path of a hunter armed with a shotgun. In such a situation, the owl may very well find himself minus some pretty feathers of his tail; and for more days than he will like, he will be extracting small pellets from his body.

   There is a moral, I guess, to all of the above which might be to the effect that he who ventures forth upon new and unfamiliar paths should at least take the precaution of knowing where they may very well lead.

THE OWL (continued)

THE PRIZE 36

PREVIEW WORDS

whatever reward result endeavors prize legion decide ourselves whether effort climb greased bedside patient noble children strive behavior piece higher students greater accuracy typewriting achieve important mastery football basketball baseball improve contests sports goals

WORDS

Whatever may be the reward that comes to us as the result of any	14	337
of our endeavors, that is the prize. No matter how many kinds of	27	350
efforts there may be (and their names are legion) there must also be just	42	365
as many prizes. The only thing that each of us must decide for	54	377
ourselves is whether the prize we seek is worth the effort we make.	68	391
I have seen a man climb a greased pole to get a straw hat that	81	404
was on top of that pole. I have seen a doctor work all night at the	95	418
bedside of a patient in order that in the morning she might claim the	109	432
prize of a human life. That is indeed a noble prize. There are children	124	447
who strive the whole day long to be on their best behavior in order	137	460
that they might receive a piece of cake at suppertime. I have seen	151	474
many students strive each day to achieve higher speeds and greater	164	487
accuracy in typewriting to achieve the prize of a good grade in the	178	501
course.	180	503
One of the most important parts of almost every major paper in	193	516
this country is the sports section. On those pages, you will find stories	208	531
of contests of all kinds—contests in which men and women strive for	222	545
the mastery and for the sake of all the prizes which go to the winners.	237	560
Golf, tennis, football, basketball, baseball, and a long list of other sports,	252	575
have their followers. The team and all the members put forth their	266	589
best efforts, day in and day out, to win prizes of all sorts.	279	602
The person who learns early in life the value of setting goals and	293	616
never losing sight of those goals is the person who wins most of the	307	630
prizes. Keep that in mind each day as you try to improve your skill	321	644
in all areas.	324	647

| 1 | 2 | 3 | 4 | 5 | 6 | 7 | 8 | 9 | 10 | 11 | 12 | 13 | 14 |

THE WINNER (continued)

A NEED TO CHANGE

55

PREVIEW WORDS

owl somber hollow trunk contented dwelt wily thief bandits of the woods gradually accumulated wisdom lofty aerial perch pondering over unknown limited imperfect embarrassed discontented aloof lads and follies world generation fluttered duffer Noah jeering upsetting options noticeable

	WORDS

There was once an owl, somber of color and sober of manner, who lived high up in the hollow trunk of a giant oak tree. He was happy and contented; and warmed by the sun and lighted by the moon, he dwelt there in comfort, safe and secure from that wily thief, the fox, and from all other bandits of the woods.

As the years went by, he gradually accumulated a store of wisdom, or at least something that seemed to him to be such. Now and then, though, as he gazed out of the window of his lofty aerial perch, he found himself pondering over the unknown that might possibly lie beyond the edge of his limited and imperfect vision. At length, there grew up within him a strong temptation that embarrassed him and made him discontented.

He had selected the spot were he resided with the idea of holding himself aloof from the fads and follies of the world, but every now and then he would catch a glimpse of the younger generation of owls as they fluttered from branch to branch. He could hear their remarks as they mocked and jeered, asking one another who the old duffer was, anyhow, and saying that he must be older than Noah and just about ready to die.

The jeering of the young owls was very upsetting to him, and he shut his door and window and sat down to consider his options. He could stay in his house, he reasoned; or he could go out to the young owls and take a role of leadership among them, or he could make a dramatic and very noticeable change in his life-style which would make the young owls take proper notice.

(continued)

| 1 | 2 | 3 | 4 | 5 | 6 | 7 | 8 | 9 | 10 | 11 | 12 | 13 | 14 |

THE OWL

55

GOALS AND PERFORMANCE 37

PREVIEW WORDS

although value shoulder briefly study reflected lives those successful useful about failures avoid shape perhaps examples persons ourselves women respect accomplishment uttered personality practical tackling factors degree halfhearted glamorous condition attainment naturally

WORDS

Although there is little value in looking over our shoulders more than briefly, just to see where we have been, we may learn much from a study of the past. A look at the past as it is reflected in the lives of those about us who have become successful can be useful. Much can be learned from those about us who have become failures, too; at least we can learn some of the things we might wish to avoid doing as our lives take shape.

Most of us have heard of, and even perhaps have met, living examples of both types of persons—those who have been successful and those who have not—and we know and can judge for ourselves from the lives of these people. We know that the men or women who call forth our highest respect do so more through what they have accomplished in life than by mere words they have uttered, or by what is often called their "good personalities."

We live in an essentially practical age in which goals and performance count more than personality, although there is little question that good personal characteristics are important factors in our lives. When you stop to think about it, though, you know that nobody has ever reached any degree of success by sitting and waiting for it or by tackling a job in a halfhearted way or simply by being charming.

Success is rarely a gift; for most of us, it is a condition that has to be earned. It will come easier if we do not think of success as our goal but rather as a condition that comes with our attainment of goals. In plain words, success is a possibility for all of us if we know that it comes naturally to all who set desirable goals and achieve them.

(continued)

| 1 | 2 | 3 | 4 | 5 | 6 | 7 | 8 | 9 | 10 | 11 | 12 | 13 | 14 |

TWO SURE THINGS   54

PREVIEW WORDS

surest perfect failure inmost soul breath of life self-esteem continued attempt knowledge trouble signboard labeled straight line shortest two between yourself utter reach variety scenery count strong can generally instruction naturally difference genuine prize litter of kittens cats

WORDS

One of the surest means of making a perfect failure is to know too much, which does not mean that you need to know things which are not so. When you enter upon your first position, you may in your inmost soul believe that you know more about the details of your work than the wisest boss that ever drew the breath of life. It may be true, of course, and the little self-esteem contained in the idea will not hurt you so long as you keep it to yourself. It is when you attempt to air that knowledge that you get into trouble with the person higher up than you are.

The signboard labeled "mistakes" indicates a road to failure which is not at all bad. We have been told that a straight line is the shortest distance between two points. If that is true, then the road of mistakes is about as straight a line as could be drawn between yourself and utter failure, and it does not take a long time to reach the end of it. It may be a surer way of failing than the practice of knowing too much, but it is shorter and has more variety in the way of scenery. The desire to tell you and the world how to make mistakes that count is strong, but it has been found that good mistakes can generally be made without any instruction. In fact they come naturally to most people, and it does not make much difference what brand they adopt, the result is the same.

If you think of all the ways there are to achieve genuine failure, you will know that making mistakes takes the prize simply because there are so many kinds. Like a litter of kittens, they are all alike and yet all different. No matter, they all grow up into cats in the end.

|1 |2 |3 |4 |5 |6 |7 |8 |9 |10 |11 |12 |13 |14

FAILURE (continued)

SUCCESS AND THE TECHNIQUE OF LIVING

38

PREVIEW WORDS

nonsense success associate power authority ability acquire prosperity occupy positions obtained degree themselves question really incidental issues sense chief ambition outward public private achievement worth seriously studying technique grown realize coupled wordly inevitable

WORDS

A great deal of nonsense has been talked and written about success, and a good many people have come to associate success with a sense of power and authority over others, as well as the ability to acquire material comfort and prosperity. It is probably true that those who have made a success of their lives have come to occupy positions of power and authority and also have obtained some comfort and a degree of wealth for themselves. This latter, though, does not of itself spell success. It is an important fact, without question, that the power and wealth are really incidental. They are not the main issues in any sense at all.

The chief, and probably the sole, ambition of these very successful people was to make the most of their own abilities, to get the best out of themselves and out of life. Their outward success, which is apparent to all, is simply the public proof of a private achievement worth ever so much more than the money wealth. It is an achievement that is the well earned reward of those who seriously set about studying what we may call the technique of living. For it is a truth, that all of us who have grown up realize, that the development of self, when coupled with self-discipline, makes wordly success inevitable. There always has been and there always will be plenty of room at the top.

So, let us think of a few things that might help us on our way. Let us think this idea through, and then let us give some time to planning the actions that we shall take in order to make our future as pleasant as and perhaps more pleasant than our present. We have nothing to lose.

| 1 | 2 | 3 | 4 | 5 | 6 | 7 | 8 | 9 | 10 | 11 | 12 | 13 | 14 |

SUCCESS *(continued)*

THE OVERSIGHT 53

PREVIEW WORDS

subject of failure received attention ancient writers notice somebody prophets carefully Bible advice difficult understand oversight respect touched worthy astonishing ideas Noah zoo Elijah flying machine skipped example studied writings related Old Testament possessed first-class

It seems to me that the subject of failure has never received the attention it may deserve. In looking back over the works of ancient writers, you will find that this is the one thing they have passed over without notice, maybe because they wanted to leave something for somebody else to think and write about. The prophets do not mention failure, and folks who have looked carefully through the Bible say they have not found the word, much less any advice upon the subject.

It is somehow difficult to understand the oversight with respect to failure, for the writers who wrote the books for the Bible seem to have touched on almost every other text worthy of any kind of note including some quite astonishing ideas. Noah was a man ahead of the times with his scheme of shipbuilding and his plan for a zoo. Elijah had some very good ideas about the building of a flying machine. But when it comes to our topic, failure, the authors of the books simply skipped it, although it is related by those who have studied the writings, that there are plenty of examples, and good ones, of failures in the Old Testament.

It seems to some folks that this dodging a subject which is filled to the brim with vast possibilities has been such a wrong to the human race that it ought to be set right at once. That may be the case, but there are a good many people throughout history who seem to have bent every energy they possessed toward making a first-class failure and who have furnished shining examples of what can be done even without advice. Maybe they could have had bigger failures if they had been told how.

(continued)

FAILURE

CAREFREE DAYS OF SUMMER

39

PREVIEW WORDS

although score tow-headed worry myself carefree patches trousers
originally occur society considered circles coated walking slowly
kicking leaving swinging instructions pasture blueberries shortcake
errand reason specifications whistling important finally summer

WORDS

It was only a few years ago—at any rate, that is the way it seems 14
to me, although three score and ten years have passed since that time 28
long ago—that I was a small tow-headed boy, having nothing on my 41
mind to worry about except my cap and my hair. 51

As I look back, I see myself happy and carefree, careless of the 65
fact that the patches on my trousers covered a much larger area than 78
did the goods from which they were originally made. Nor did it occur 92
to me in those days that shirts and ties should be worn in good 105
society and that to go without shoes and socks was not considered 118
good form in the best circles. I never wore them in hot weather, and 132
my legs were coated with a tan the likes of which any sun worshiper 146
would be proud. 150

I can see myself walking slowly along the dusty road on a hot 163
July day, kicking up the dust with my toes and leaving clouds of it 177
behind me as I went. Swinging in my hand would be a large pail 189
which had been given to me by my mother with instructions to hurry 203
down to the pasture where the blueberries grew. I was to pick a pail 217
full and be home in time for supper. She was making the shortcake 230
to go with the berries. 236

It was the first time I had been sent on an errand of that kind, 250
but I saw no good reason why I could not live up to the specifications 264
in every detail. So I started off, whistling as I went, and finally came 279
to the berry field. The bushes were fairly blue with berries, and as I 293
picked, I could hear them as they dropped on the bottom of the pail. 307
I liked the sound for it made me feel very important and grown up. 321

(continued)

| 1 | 2 | 3 | 4 | 5 | 6 | 7 | 8 | 9 | 10 | 11 | 12 | 13 | 14 |

BALSA, THE INSULATOR

52

PREVIEW WORDS

strong rays immediately insulating balsa tree maximum dead air possible resistance moisture ninety-two woodiness condensation is eliminated relation weight standpoint construction waterproofed less effectiveness highly resilient tight-fitting joints prevents leakage cork resembles

When we think about trees, the idea of shade from the strong rays of the sun comes immediately to mind. We do not very often think about the trees as a source of supply for insulating products. It is a matter of some importance, however, that the balsa tree has been used to insulate. Please understand, of course, that it is the wood of the balsa tree about which we are thinking rather than the quite unusual tree itself.

A good insulant always includes a maximum amount of dead air in the smallest possible units and must also offer good resistance to moisture. Balsa tree wood meets these requirements quite handily. When thoroughly dry, balsa contains about ninety-two per cent dead air with almost no woodiness. As a result, little air enters the pores; and, therefore, condensation is eliminated. Its unusual strength in relation to its weight also makes balsa an ideal insulant from the standpoint of most construction. It is very easily handled and is more satisfactorily waterproofed than many other insulants of similar or less effectiveness.

Being highly resilient, balsa assures tight-fitting joints and, as a result, prevents leakage due to strain. In addition, when kiln-dried and waterproofed, balsa will not normally crack or crumble. Another point about it is that balsa, dried in the kiln, is completely sanitary and odorless. Unlike cork, which it most nearly resembles in weight, balsa does not have to be fitted together in small pieces to cover large areas. Instead it can be used in fairly large panels. It can be milled and shaped with ordinary woodworking tools, which is another important advantage.

BALSA (continued)

A SMALL BOY AND BLUEBERRIES

40

PREVIEW WORDS

picking sunny blueberries speed covered bigger wondered singing music filtered drowsy surely fallen saucy chipmunk understand language harm message insult instant scurry cuckoo nearby afraid deprive butterfly yellow blossom guessed assure slowly clover glanced naturally visits

WORDS

    The day was warm and sunny, and I set about picking blueberries with speed. After a while, I glanced in the pail and saw that the bottom was not even covered. Each time I put in another berry, it seemed to me that the pail grew bigger and bigger. The more berries I picked, the more I wondered if I would ever fill it, one at a time.

    On every side the birds were singing; and the soft wind made music as it filtered through the tree tops. I became drowsy and would have surely fallen asleep had it not been for a saucy little chipmunk that came out from under a rock and began to talk to me. Naturally, there was no way I could understand his language, but I got the message that he wanted me to go away. Now, this was an insult no small boy could stand for an instant, so I had to get up and toss some stones at him. I did not hit him. In fact, I am pretty sure I did not want to harm him at all, but he did scurry back to his hole and leave me alone.

    After a while, a cuckoo flew into a nearby bush, and she looked at me and also began talking to me. I guess she was afraid I was going to deprive her of her share of the blueberries. A little while later, a big yellow butterfly lit on a nearby clover blossom. Naturally, I had to catch her, for no boy would miss a chance like that. With the visits from the chipmunk and the cuckoo and the butterfly, you know I was not picking many blueberries, and my pail got bigger all the time.

    You guessed it—I forgot all about picking those blueberries. I can assure you there was fear in my heart as I slowly walked home.

| 1 | 2 | 3 | 4 | 5 | 6 | 7 | 8 | 9 | 10 | 11 | 12 | 13 | 14 |

SUMMER *(continued)*

BALSA, THE LIGHTEST WOOD

PREVIEW WORDS

model airplane lightest wood basic material balsa popular bombax trees American tropics Ecuador forests plantations water courses rich moisture thrives possessed unusual strength cork brittle commercial pounds cubic drying kilns exporting extensive covered sheds remilled thickness plants

Years ago, and it is still true to some extent today, model airplane builders made their flying models out of the lightest wood in the world. And if you are going to build anything in which the basic material must be both light and soft, the lightest wood in the world, balsa, may be your best buy. It is popular still and not only with model makers.

The balsa tree is from the bombax family of trees which are found chiefly in the American tropics in or near Ecuador. Almost all of the balsa in the world comes from that country. It is found in forests, on plantations, and along water courses where there is rich soil with lots of moisture. It thrives in damp places; and so, as you might expect, the tropics provide a healthy home for the bombax trees. The more rapidly balsa grows, the lighter and softer it is; so it is valuable as a soft wood, possessed of unusual strength for its light weight. Lighter than cork and less brittle, commercial balsa weighs six to fifteen pounds per cubic foot which means that it averages under ten pounds when dry.

After leaving the drying kilns of the exporting company in Ecuador, balsa is transported by means of an extensive system of tracks and some transfer cars to large covered sheds for storage. It is remilled here and graded according to an established set of rules. Planks of the same grade, the same thickness, and the same length are tied in large bundles ranging up to fourteen feet in length. There are five to nine layers of these planks in a bundle. Such an arrangement allows for easy handling of balsa shipment to receiving ports all over the world.

(continued)

BALSA

FIRST THERE WAS SNOW ICE

PREVIEW WORDS

don't suppose invented certainly ought somebody America's favorite Rome emperors catered palates fleet mountains mixed honey wonder happened runner brought power harsh snow-ice traced custom Marco Polo frozen Swiss description recipe liquids flask naturalist delicacies confined masses

I don't suppose that we will ever know who invented ice cream, but we certainly ought to give somebody credit for it, for we can all agree that ice cream has always been one of America's favorite foods.

When Rome was in its glory, emperors were men to be catered to, and every new day had to bring forth something new for the palates of the emperor and his friends. The story is told that during this time, men who were fleet of foot sped up the mountains and brought down some snow which they mixed with honey and fruit juices. Do you wonder what would have happened had the emperor been late for dinner and the hard snow melted, or if the runner was not so fast as he might have been and then brought home water that had once been snow? In those days, the men in power had rather harsh ways of treating people who did not please them.

The idea for this snow-ice that the emperors of Rome enjoyed so much can be traced to an even earlier period of history. In the East, it was a custom to mix the snow with wines. Perhaps it was Marco Polo who brought back from his long stay in the East a description of the frozen food and a recipe for making it, too. From a later period of history, we read reports that liquids were frozen by packing a filled flask and keeping it in motion until the liquid was frozen. A Swiss naturalist describes in some detail a process used very early in his country as "shaking milk in jars and hardening it by cold." Such delicacies as ice cream were, of course, confined to the Court and to the very rich. Many years would pass before the masses could afford to buy ice cream.

(continued)

ICE CREAM

MORE ABOUT THE SUPPLIES DEPARTMENT

50

PREVIEW WORDS

employed early six days basement basket delivered sales books provided six inches wide size allowed stacks handle strong fellow details learned location departments charge duty picked stored future reference first business responsibility supplies stuff stock requisitions accountant

WORDS

    The store in which I had been employed opened at a very early hour each morning, six days a week. The first thing I did was to go to the basement and get the basket with which I delivered and picked up the sales books. The basket that was provided was about three feet long, six inches wide, and less than thirty inches high. This size allowed us to place the books in three stacks. The books were rather heavy to handle, but I would not let on that I was not every bit as strong as the next fellow. After doing this job for a few days, I got to know the details, and learned the location of many departments and the names of the men who were in charge of things. I was soon put in charge of this work and the duty of seeing that the sales books were put in place each day and the old ones picked up and stored away for future reference. I felt it was my first real business responsibility, and I was proud.

    I kept on the job for awhile, and we added to our staff; and another lad followed me to do the things that I used to do. I went into another room where the supplies were kept and took my place alongside the other fellows to issue what was called for by the departments in the store.

    In the morning there was a rush for supplies, and we worked at top speed giving out the stuff to those who came for it. When the rush was over, we had to check stock and report to the chief so that he could order from the salesmen who called about that time. Our next job was to learn the prices and later price the requisitions which were sent to the accountant so that the departments could be charged.

| 1 | 2 | 3 | 4 | 5 | 6 | 7 | 8 | 9 | 10 | 11 | 12 | 13 | 14 |

THE SUPPLIES DEPARTMENT *(continued)*   **50**

THEN THERE WAS ICE CREAM   42

PREVIEW WORDS

Paris Florence sherbets devised recipe contained manuscript document suppose biggest gratitude French colonists brought formula operated pastry America machine invented George Washington Thomas Jefferson diary collection official Dolly Madison probably inaugural delicacy

Many years after the Roman emperors mixed snow with honey and juices, a cafe was opened in Paris by a man from Florence. There is some reason to believe that he might have used milk as well as fruit juices in some of his sherbets. However, it was some time later before cream ice was devised. The recipe was contained in a manuscript found in France, and the title of this document was "The Art of Making Ice."

I suppose that we in America owe the biggest debt of gratitude for ice cream to the French, for it was some French colonists who brought to this country a formula for the making of ice cream. They were the ones who operated pastry shops and made and sold ice cream as part of their business. America was not very old when a machine was invented and sold for people to make ice cream at home. George Washington made notes in his diary about a purchase of one of these machines, but his wife's collection of recipes does not include one for making ice cream. However, Thomas Jefferson wrote many recipes for it.

You might think that either Washington or Jefferson should be given credit for being the first to serve ice cream on the official table, but this honor has been given to Dolly Madison. She probably was the first hostess to serve the delicacy at a large assembly. It was reported by newspapers covering the event that large domes of pink ice cream were served at the second inaugural ball, and the dessert was a hit.

The invention of the hand-crank freezer was a welcome innovation. Without it, we would not enjoy ice cream as we know it today.

ICE CREAM *(continued)*

THE SUPPLIES DEPARTMENT   49

PREVIEW WORDS

decided touch dad's former customers club father matter chance getting store opened position head departments openings young lad apparently interview application many questions answered filled form high hopes exciting packing paper invoices conduct mornings special basement task

	WORDS
Many years ago, when I was very young, I decided that it would	13
be best for me to go out and get a job away from home. I got in	26
touch with one of my dad's former customers. This man used to come	40
to the club which my father ran and became a friend of ours—and	53
still is for that matter. I asked him if there was any chance of my	66
getting a job in the large, new store that had been opened in town	80
and in which he had a position as the head of one of the departments.	94
He said he would find out if there were any openings for a young	107
lad, which he did right away, apparently.	116
It was only a few days later that I saw him again, and he told	129
me to go to the store for an interview and to fill out an application.	144
So I went to the store and there they asked me many questions, and	157
I answered all I could. I filled in the form they gave me and went	171
home with high hopes of entering a new world.	180
The following Monday morning I was at work at the new job. It	193
was in the supplies department of the store which kept the store	206
furnished with packing paper, invoices, and in fact, everything that is	221
used in the conduct of the business. There was a small cage, as we	234
used to call it, in the basement that was filled with sales books, new	248
and old, that the people who sold goods used. In the mornings it was	262
my job to take the new books to a special place on each floor and	275
deliver them for the work of the day. At the same places where I left	290
the new books, it was my job to pick up the old ones and return	302
them to the basement of the store. It may seem a simple task, but it	316
was one which I liked.	322

(continued)

| 1 | 2 | 3 | 4 | 5 | 6 | 7 | 8 | 9 | 10 | 11 | 12 | 13 | 14 |

RULES OF THE ROAD

43

PREVIEW WORDS

rented England London delivered renting completion notify arrangement agent around anything necessary different instead gearshift remember left-hand brought wasted interesting excellent appreciated courtesy hurried downstairs carrying contained British Highway Code Golden Rule

	WORDS
A few years ago, a good friend and I rented a car to tour the	13
south of England. We were to pick up the car in front of our hotel	27
in London where it would be delivered to us by the renting agent.	40
Upon completion of the trip, we were to notify him; and he would	53
come for it and pick it up at the same spot. This was a very nice	66
arrangement.	70
When the call came that our car was ready, I hurried downstairs,	84
leaving my friend in the room. Out in front of the hotel I saw the	97
small car that I was going to drive. My friend was to act as guide.	112
The agent and I drove around for a while so that I might get used	126
to the car and also that I might learn anything that was necessary to	140
know about it that was different from my own car at home. The driver	154
of the English car sits on the right instead of on the left; the gearshift	169
on this car was on my left instead of my right; and, of course, I had	183
to remember that we were to drive on the left-hand side of the road.	197
By the time we got the car back in front of the hotel, my friend	211
had brought our bags down and we wasted no time in getting on our	224
way on what turned out to be one of the most interesting and enjoyable	238
holidays we have ever had. It was May and the weather was nice and	252
brisk, ideal for touring. The roads were in excellent condition, and we	266
appreciated the courtesy shown us by other drivers. Perhaps they had	280
been reading, and I know they were carrying out the spirit of the	293
rules of the road contained in the British Highway Code. This code	307
expresses the belief that roads will be safer when drivers practice the	321
Golden Rule.	325

(continued)

| 1 | 2 | 3 | 4 | 5 | 6 | 7 | 8 | 9 | 10 | 11 | 12 | 13 | 14 |

MORE ON THE MANAGEMENT GAME

48

PREVIEW WORDS

management ownership profession chiefly interest characteristic people willingness obligation binding operation titles meddling principles ebb social political fashions affected regulations permanent kind occupation excuses alibis forces compel demonstrate convince persuade earns skill

WORDS

There have been times, perhaps not so long ago, when management	13 340
and ownership meant almost the same thing. Today the profession of	27 354
management is made up chiefly of people whose interest is not in	40 367
ownership but in seeing why and how a job should be done. The	53 380
characteristic of such people, of course, is their willingness to be	66 393
responsible. And I will say that those who do not feel that obligation	81 408
binding upon them or who fail to live up to it are not managing an	94 421
operation no matter what the titles of their jobs may be. They may	108 435
only be meddling.	112 439
Most principles of management are bigger than the ebb and flow	125 452
of social and political fashion and cannot be thought of as being greatly	140 467
affected by them. True principles never change. It is only the conditions	155 482
under which management always must be exercised that change. The	168 495
technique and ability of management must adapt. The responsibility that	183 510
goes with management is not a conditional thing to be laid aside with	197 524
the advent of a difficult set of regulations. The responsibility is full	212 539
and permanent, and when it is gone, management may be gone too.	225 552
My point is really that management is the kind of occupation in	238 565
which excuses and alibis do not go. There is no time out in that	252 579
game, no matter how the rules or conditions may change. Either	264 591
management is managing, or it is not. Over the long pull, however,	278 605
management cannot force or compel. It has to demonstrate, to convince,	292 619
to persuade; and to do these things, it must be right more often than	306 633
wrong. Management has no rights other than those it earns through	320 647
demonstrations of skill.	325 652

| 1 | 2 | 3 | 4 | 5 | 6 | 7 | 8 | 9 | 10 | 11 | 12 | 13 | 14 |

THE MANAGEMENT GAME *(continued)*

DO UNTO OTHERS

44

PREVIEW WORDS

thought forget hog highway suggests conduct standard common interest welfare demands conform respect spirit underlying habit courtesy wasn't accidents addition allowance possible alertness caution affected alcohol fatigue fraction avoiding winding hospital prematurely epitaph competition

	WORDS	
I like the thought about making the roads safer for others, for it	14	339
points out a fact that some people seem to forget when they drive at	28	353
very fast speeds, cut in and out of line, or hog the road. The Code	42	367
points out that others use the highway and have the same rights as	55	380
you have. It suggests a standard of conduct in the common interest,	69	394
and our own welfare demands that all of us conform to it. Respect for	83	408
the Code, therefore, as well as for the spirit underlying it is so much	98	423
a moral duty that its practice must become a habit of real courtesy.	113	438
Accidents will happen, the Code warns, unless in addition to our	127	452
own careful driving we make extra allowance for possible errors on the	141	466
part of other drivers. We must be sure that our own alertness or sense	151	480
of caution is not affected by alcohol or drugs or fatigue before we use	170	495
the roads. A fraction of a second may be the difference between	183	508
avoiding an accident and winding up in a hospital bed. It may be the	197	522
difference between continuing a happy life on earth or going into the	211	536
next one a bit prematurely. Even if you do have the right of way, it	225	550
is not always wise to take it. Think of the epitaph on the grave of	238	563
one young driver, "I had the right of way, and I took it." Silly of	252	577
him, wasn't it?	256	581
The Highway Code repeats over and over again that you have	268	593
duties toward other drivers on the road, and it suggests that you do	282	607
not drive in a spirit of competition with them. It does not pay. It is	297	622
too much of a hazard. The Code asks you never to forget to do unto	310	635
other drivers as you would have other drivers do unto you. That is	324	649
good advice.	327	652

| 1 | 2 | 3 | 4 | 5 | 6 | 7 | 8 | 9 | 10 | 11 | 12 | 13 | 14 |

RULES OF THE ROAD (continued)

THE MANAGEMENT GAME

PREVIEW WORDS

business remember improve operations responsible simple recognize third occurred increasing difficulty anyone readily process recognition action manager details sufficiently aggressive sense strongly importance assume direction decisions consequences comparison football signals captains

	WORDS
At an early stage in my business career, I can remember being	13
told that the way to improve the operations for which I was responsible	27
was very simple. I must learn to recognize a problem when I had one	41
and decide what needed to be done to meet it. The third step was	54
to do what had to be done in order to improve the operation. I was	68
also informed that these steps occurred in order of increasing difficulty.	83
I was told that anyone who was alive and had his eyes open could	96
readily recognize a problem. That was the easy part of the process, to	111
be sure.	113
Something more than recognition, however, is required. A person	127
has to go on from there to the second step. One has to decide what	140
is to be done. To put the decision into action requires not only the	154
manager but also the people who will carry out the details. The	167
problem of the manager, therefore, is not confined simply to recognizing	182
the problem.	185
In the broad sense, management must be made up of those people	198
who are sufficiently aggressive and have enough sense of responsibility	213
to mind not only their own business but also the business of other	226
people. They feel strongly enough about the importance of having things	241
done right that they are willing to assume the direction of them. They	255
do things because of this feeling rather than just for the money. They	269
are willing to see action taken on their decisions, and if trouble comes,	284
they are willing to take the consequences. To make a comparison with	298
football, they call signals on offense and hold the safety job on the	312
defense. Like captains, they encourage others to successful action.	327

(continued)

| 1 | 2 | 3 | 4 | 5 | 6 | 7 | 8 | 9 | 10 | 11 | 12 | 13 | 14 |

TAKE FOUR CUPS OF FLOUR   45

PREVIEW WORDS

animals grain tasty boiled pounding powder mixing mixture milling
baking industries beginnings crude experiments yeast rising secrets
yesterday tombs Egypt dough Bible carried leavened kneading troughs
England quantities official coarse celebrations royalty prized Greeks

WORDS

    We are not certain how the use of grain for making bread started. Perhaps man noticed the animals eating grain and thought that he would try it himself. Maybe he tried to chew the grain but found it not as tasty as he would like and decided to try it boiled in water. Then one day, he may have hit upon the idea of pounding the grain into a powder, mixing the powder with water, and baking the mixture with the heat of his fire. I have read somewhere that it is most likely that our great milling and baking industries had their beginnings in these simple and often crude experiments of man, many years ago.

    Just when yeast began to play a rising part in the process is not known and is one of the secrets hidden in the years of yesterday. In one of the tombs found in Egypt some years ago, pictures showing grain being ground, yeast being made, and dough being mixed and baked were found. The Bible tells us that as a certain group of people left Egypt, they carried with them dough before it was leavened and their kneading troughs, so as to be sure of an ample supply of the staff of life.

    Many of the countries near Egypt adopted Egyptian methods of making bread. The Greeks, for instance, became famed for their fine breads and rolls of many types; and when their land was overrun, their bakers were among the most highly prized slaves of all who were captured.

    In England each great manor had its own bakehouse, but the bread they baked was coarse. The small quantities of fine white bread that were made were held for special official celebrations of the royalty.

(continued)

| 1 | 2 | 3 | 4 | 5 | 6 | 7 | 8 | 9 | 10 | 11 | 12 | 13 | 14 |

BREAD

THEN ADD SOME YEAST

PREVIEW WORDS

native colonists sown enjoyed supplement cornbread methods farmers
treatment sifted housewives available factors responsible reaping
quite yeast bread-making industries invention grinding friction
century commercial cleanliness pastry consistent quality affected

You may know that wheat is not a native product of America. It	13	335
was first brought here by the colonists. As soon as the ground was	27	349
cleared, the seeds were sown; and it was not very long before the	40	362
people enjoyed wheat bread as a supplement to the cornbread made	53	375
from the native grain.	58	380
Milling and baking methods in this country were the same as those	72	394
used in the mother country. Farmers raised their grains, took them to	86	408
a mill, and waited for them to be ground. Quite often the meal was	100	422
used without any more treatment, but some of it was sifted and resifted	114	436
to make a finer flour. The flour was brought to the housewives, for	128	450
bread made at home was the only kind available in the early days.	141	463
Two factors are largely responsible for the development of the huge	155	477
milling and bread-making industries of today. One is the invention of	169	491
the reaping machine; the other, the invention of grinding machinery.	183	505
Today both hard and soft wheat can be ground without friction by	196	518
modern grinding machines. The heat from friction made by the older	210	532
grinding stones affected the quality of the flour. Now the large mills	224	546
are able to buy various types of wheat and blend them in such a way	238	560
that flour will be consistent in quality. Flour made from soft wheat is	253	575
known as pastry flour and is used for breads that are not raised with	267	589
yeast.	269	591
Cleanliness is important in baking and delivering bread and other	283	605
products made of flour. The wrapping of loaves in paper only became	297	619
a common practice in this century. Today commercial baking ranks	310	632
among the largest of all food industries.	319	641

| 1 | 2 | 3 | 4 | 5 | 6 | 7 | 8 | 9 | 10 | 11 | 12 | 13 | 14 |

BREAD (continued)